Egypt

The
Business Traveller's
Handbook

Egypt
The Business Traveller's Handbook

published by
Gorilla Guides
128 Kensington Church Street
London W8 4BH
Tel: 44 20 7221 7166   Fax: 44 20 7792 9288
E-mail: stacey.international@virgin.net

ISBN: 1 903185 00 9

CIP Data: A catalogue record for this book is available from the British Library

© Gorilla Guides 2000

Series Editor: Max Scott
Editor (Egypt): Hugh Davies
Production: Kitty Carruthers & Sam Crooks
Design: Nimbus Design
Printing & Binding: Tien Wah Press, Singapore

The author and publisher have made every effort to ensure that the facts in this handbook are accurate and up-to-date. The reader is recommended, however, to verify travel and visa arrangements with a suitable consular office or airline agent before departure. The author and publisher cannot accept any responsibility for loss, injury or inconvenience, however caused.

None of the maps in this book are designed to have any political significance.

PICTURE CREDITS: *Title page,* Stuart Turpin (ffotograff); *page 4 (l)* Mike Gerard (ffotograff), *(tr)* Melissa Shales, (ffotograff), *(m & br)* Mark Hannaford (ffotograff); page 5 *(t)* Alan Ward (ffotograff), *(b)* Stuart Turpin (ffotograff); page 6, Michael Barron; *page 7,* Catherine May; *page 8,* Alan Ward (ffotograff).

Egypt

The Business Traveller's Handbook

James Lawday

Far left: A guide rests in the shade of the Temple of Luxor.

Top left: A snake charmer confidently grasps a cobra at Luxor cattle market.

Middle left: The ruins of Philae Temple of Mathor in Aswan.

Bottom left: The Soviet-built monument to Aswan Dam project.

Above: Cairo's skyscrapers overlooking the Nile, seen from the air.

Below: A local woman resists the tempting goods on offer at a roadside store in Luxor.

Traders go about their business in a time-honoured way outside Bab Zuwayla in Cairo (above), while, in a more tranquil setting, residents return home to their houseboats on the bank of the Nile by Imbaba (right).

Acknowledgements

I would like to thank the many people who have unwittingly supplied me with information about Egypt over the last fifteen years since I became involved with the country, people who have given me a greater understanding of this fascinating country – the taxi drivers, the senior businessmen, the boabs, the diplomats and the government officials in the UK and Egypt.

I should thank Antonia and the family for their help and support in these years whilst we have lived, sometimes in difficult circumstances, in the Middle East and John Laing International who have enabled me to experience Egypt.

JL August 2000

CONTENTS

FOREWORD

by Sir David Blatherwick
Chairman of the Egyptian British Chamber of Commerce
and former British Ambassador to Egypt

James Lawday is a senior member of the British business community in Cairo, long resident there. This book reflects his deep knowledge of local conditions in Egypt, his profound common sense, and his dry humour. It is stuffed with information on how to get there, where to stay and – most important – where to get good advice. Even the regular visitor, or the resident businessman, will find something to learn from it. Egypt is not one of those countries where visiting businessmen can breeze in, do a quick deal and breeze out again. It requires commitment, repeated visits and patience. And it needs homework before you set out, and when you get back.

But the rewards are commensurate. Egypt has a large population, about 65 million (half the Arab world) and a large and sophisticated middle class – perhaps 10 to 15 million people. Thanks to the economic policies followed since the early 1990s inflation is low, growth high and the budget deficit is below 2 per cent of GDP. Foreign debt is minimal and the reserves stand at nearly a year's imports. As a result of the privatisation programme, over 70 per cent of GDP now comes from the private sector. The economy is widely based with good hard currency earnings.

Egypt has long been a producer of oil. But gas finds over the last few years have changed the picture radically. Egypt is set to become one of the world's top five gas producers, and even after domestic needs are fully met, most will be available for export. Plans are well under way to export to the eastern Mediterranean countries, to Turkey and to Europe.

Egyptians buy pretty much everything exporters have to offer, from machinery to financial services, from chemicals to consultancies. Britain is now the biggest foreign (i.e. non-Arab) investor in Egypt, just ahead of the USA. Some 200 American firms and 190 British firms operate there, including many of our major companies. There is ample room for more.

Whatever your business, you will find this book a useful guide.

DB

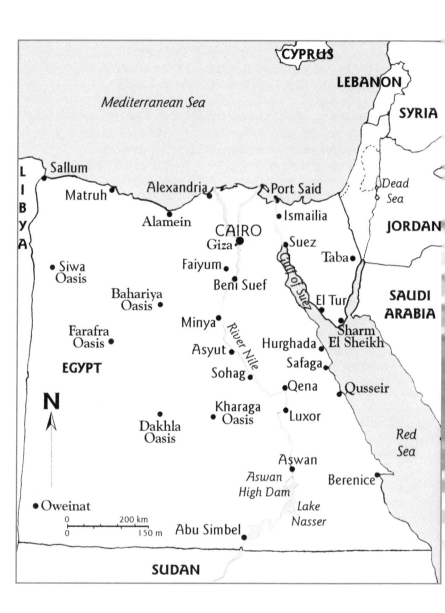

The Arab Republic of Egypt

1

Egypt yesterday and today

Egypt yesterday and today

1

A bird's-eye view of the nation, and the special features that distinguish it from other countries.

A condensed history.

The modern country.

Overview of a Nation

Egypt is a unique country containing a large proportion of the world's archaeological remains. In recent history Egypt has been influenced by one foreign civilisation after another. Russia, Britain, France and Turkey have all affected the country in various ways. Britain developed the current bureaucracy, Russia left a legacy of socialism, France influenced its legal system and Turkey bequeathed in Egypt considerable traces of its culture.

Egypt is the most densely populated country in the Arabic-speaking world and the second most populous in Africa after Nigeria. The area of Egypt is about one million square kilometres, about four times that of the UK, yet 98 per cent of its 63 million people live in about 5 per cent of the country's area, the Nile river valley and its delta. In some places there are over 1,500 people per square kilometre, one of the highest population densities in the world, and estimates indicate that about 15 million people live in Cairo alone. It is believed that half the population is under twenty years old and, with a growth rate of 2 per cent, Egypt's population is expected to double in the next twenty-five years.

Egypt has a continuous recorded history of more than 5,000 years. There have been periods of strength when neighbouring territories fell under its domination punctuated by periods of weakness. Egypt was a united kingdom from about 3200 BC and first came under foreign rule in 333 BC when conquered by Alexander the Great. For the next 1,000 years the Greeks, Romans and Byzantines ruled the country, until in the middle of the seventh century the Muslim Arabs under Amr Ibn al-As arrived; Egypt has been a predominantly Muslim and Arab country ever since. The Ottoman Turk occupation began in the sixteenth century. Under Napoleon the French briefly occupied Egypt. The British came at the end of the nineteenth century, declaring Egypt a protectorate in 1914 and finally leaving in 1952. That same year a military coup led to the abdication of King Farouk, and the proclamation of a republic in 1953. Mohammed Naquib, Gamal Abdul Nasser, Anwar Sadat and today Hosni Mubarak have led the country since that time.

Geographically, Egypt is both blessed and cursed. There is a long coastline on the Red Sea and another to the

1

The Nile

north on the Mediterranean. Nature has compensated Egypt for its desert areas by providing an unusually magnificent river – the Nile. With its sources in central Africa and Ethiopia, the Nile travels thousands of kilometres through Sudan into Egypt and discharges into the Mediterranean. The Nile is one of the few major rivers of the world which flows south to north, with a prevailing wind from the north. This combination of wind and current enables the traditional sailing vessels of the river – *feluccas* – to drift on the current and return to the south under sail.

Ecology of the Nile

The dramatically ancient irrigation processes have been largely superseded by modern agricultural and transport methods. Yields on the land have increased now, so that two or three crops can be grown each year. Chemical fertilisers have now replaced the fertile silt and little flushing of canals and drains is done. The drains were originally designed to drain the land of excess water in order to prevent the build-up of salts in the soil occurring as a result of evaporation. These drains, and indeed the canals, have become polluted and blocked by water hyacinth plants. These plants are a major problem to the water and irrigation authorities, requiring constant dredging and clearance. They arrived in the system many years ago, when a gardener in Aswan threw some of these Indian plants from an ornamental water garden into the Nile.

There are other environmental problems associated with the dams. The silt brought down from the mountains of central Africa is now collecting behind the High Dam. The increased weight is giving engineers concern about the security of the dam and its associated hydro-electric generating capacity. Equally serious environmental problems occur at the other end of the river. The silt and nutrients that used to discharge into the Mediterranean from the Nile Delta were a major source of food for the fish in the area. Fish stocks off the delta have been seriously depleted. Because of this lack of flushing by fresh water each year, the seawater is encroaching into the delta region, reducing its ability to sustain crops.

1

The Nile

It was perhaps the ease of movement north and south that enabled the ancients to develop the country. Rulers could embellish their temples and palaces in Memphis (present-day Cairo) with granite and marble from Aswan, some 1,000 kilometres away. At the same time, the crops grown along the narrow strip – sometimes only 500 metres wide – either side of the river could easily be moved throughout the country.

Until the construction of the high dam at Aswan, the delta and the river valley were flooded each autumn. This covered the agricultural land with a layer of fertile river silt, and flushed out the irrigation canals and drains ready for another growing season. During this flood in Pharaonic times, while there was little to be done on the land, stone could be ferried from the quarries of Moqattam on the east bank of the Nile across the water-covered valley direct to the pyramid fields on the plateau of Giza.

A Brief History of Egypt

Unification of the lands of Egypt probably took place some 5,000 years ago during the **Archaic Period**. The kings of this era ruled the land near the border between Upper and Lower Egypt at Memphis – next to the monuments of Saqarra. This period of history lasted until the era of the **Old Kingdom** (2686–2181 BC).

The Pharaohs of the Old Kingdom are probably the first kings that have become generally familiar. Djoser (2668–2649 BC), king during the third dynasty, had the first monumental stone structure built, the Step Pyramid at Saqarra. During this dynasty an effective civil service that acknowledged the absolute power of the god-king was developed to govern the country. During the fourth dynasty (2613–2498 BC) the pyramid age began, and the great pyramids of Giza for the Kings Cheops, Chephren and Menkaure were built. The fifth dynasty (2498–2345 BC), saw the dominance of the solar cult based upon the god Ra of Heliopolis. The sixth dynasty (2345–2181 BC) ended ingloriously following a lengthy reign by Pepi II.

The **First Intermediate Period** (2181–2040 BC) included dynasties seven to eleven, and is considered an uneventful period with no notable rulers.

1

Ancient History

During the **Middle Kingdom** (2040–1782 BC), the country was reunified and foreign trade resumed. The twelfth dynasty kings Amenemhet and Senworset re-established sovereignty over Lower Nubia and also pursued land reclamation projects inside Egypt, notably in the Fayoum.

Little is known about the turbulent **Second Intermediate Period** (1782–1570 BC). Reigns were generally short during the thirteenth dynasty and senior court officials held power in the country. The fourteenth dynasty was a short-lived challenge by a separatist movement from the delta. During the fifteenth dynasty invaders from Asia, collectively known as Hyskos, conquered the delta and Nubia again broke away. The native Egyptian princes found themselves contained by the Hyskos state in the north and the hostile Nubian kingdom in the south. A Theban family, claiming descent from the thirteenth dynasty, eventually reunified the country as the seventeenth dynasty. They first established a kingdom in Upper Egypt and then progressively reduced the power of the Nubians and the Hyskos.

1

The Treasures of Tutankhamoun

The fabulous treasures discovered by Carter when he first opened the tomb of Tutankhamoun in 1924 took the world by storm and inspired the images which have become part of popular culture. It was, however, merely the legacy of a relatively minor king, and yet more fabulous hoards must have been plundered by tomb robbers over the ages and melted down for gold.

However, it wasn't until the New Kingdom (1570–1070 BC) that Ahmose I, of the eighteenth dynasty, finally expelled the Hyskos and reunified Upper and Lower Egypt. The empire which then developed extended to northern Syria, and became a major power in the region. The Egyptians' control of the trade routes to southern Africa and their ownership of Nubian gold strengthened this position. For 500 years the country prospered and famous king's names such as Thutmose and Amenhotep ruled the land: Queen Hatshepsut (1498–1483 BC) rose to become a female pharaoh; Amenhotep IV (1350–1334BC), the heretic pharaoh who became Akhenaten, tried unsuccessfully to replace worship of the god Amoun; the young Tutankhamoun (1334–1325 BC) was a relatively unimportant Pharaoh, made famous only by the modern discovery and excavation of his tomb. The nineteenth dynasty saw Rameses and Seti defending the empire against Hittites to the north and Libyans to the west. In the twentieth dynasty, Rameses III had to repel no less than three invasions. The royal treasury was seriously depleted during this period, and central government control was increasingly challenged by strong local magnates.

The next 800 years saw Egypt fragment once again. The **Third Intermediate Period** (1069–525 BC) produced no notable monarchs or major achievements by the Egyptians. Regional and foreign rulers diluted the power of the country. **The Late Period** (525–332 BC) included the invasion and brief occupation by the Persians. Their rule was unpopular and the Egyptians encouraged the Greek states in their wars against the Persian empire.

Alexander the Great (332–323 BC) was the first ruler of Egypt in the **Graeco-Roman Period** (332BC–AD 293). Alexander's nine year rule was sufficient for him to adopt local customs. He installed himself as Pharaoh and became very reliant on the oracle at Amun's temple at Siwa. Upon his death Alexander's empire was divided by his generals, with Egypt falling to Ptolemy. During the Ptolemaic dynasty Greeks displaced Egyptians in the ruling classes and the country was economically exploited. Both Greek and Egyptian gods were worshipped and significant temples were built at Edfu and Kom Ombo. It was during this dynasty that the great library at Alexandria was established. The Ptolemies were frequently at war with their neighbours and the dynasty was plagued increasingly by family quarrels. The later kings fell under the influence of Rome, and in 54 BC Julius Caesar took Alexandria. Cleopatra VII, the last of the Ptolemies, continued to rule Egypt under the protection of Caesar, to whom she bore a son, and later under Mark Anthony. Following a decisive battle with Octavian (subsequently the Emperor Augustus), Cleopatra and Mark Anthony committed suicide and Egypt became a province of Rome.

The **Byzantine Period** (AD 293–642). Following the division of the Roman empire in AD 293, Egypt came under

1

Alexander the Great

The early Christians

The Byzantine Period

the control of the eastern emperors who, from AD 330, ruled from their capital at Constantinople (Byzantium). The Byzantine period (AD 293-642) saw the spread of

Christianity Christianity in Egypt, but differences with the Roman Church led to persecution. At the Council of Chalcedon in AD 451 Rome conceded autonomy to the Copts, as the Christians of Egypt became known, who established their own patriarch in Alexandria. At the same time monastic communities were founded around the country, including the Greek Orthodox monastery of St Catherine in Sinai and the Coptic foundations of St Anthony and St Mark in the Red Sea hills. In Wadi Natroun and Sohag province more monasteries were established.

The Copts

Islam is the dominant religion of Egypt, with Sunni Muslims in the majority. The country has a civil code of law and does not follow *Shari'a* law as in some Muslim countries of the region. However, the guardians of Islam in Egypt are close observers of the workings and decrees of the Government. Copts make up a small proportion of the population. They are a Christian sect found almost exclusively in Egypt, with their own Pope resident in the country. They claim to be the original descendents of the ancient Egyptians.

The **Arabs** and **Islam** arrived in Egypt in the mid seventh century. The country was conquered in AD 640-1 by Amr Ibn al-As, the general of the Caliph Umar, second successor of the Prophet Muhammad. Al-Fustat, near

Islam present-day Cairo, became the capital, replacing Alexandria. The Ummayads and then the Abbasids from Baghdad again administered the country, until in AD 868 Ibn Tulun declared independence and established the short-lived Tulunid dynasty.

With the Abbasids' rule re-established in AD 905, Egypt was governed from Baghdad until in AD 969 the **Fatimid** era was established. A new capital, al-Qahira or Cairo, was constructed replacing the adjacent capital al-Fustat. Palaces, mosques and educational establishments, including the al-Azhar University, were built. The Fatimid period was also a great commercial and industrial era for Egypt, a time of great prosperity. The Fatimids developed plantations and industries and began exporting Egyptian products, creating a wide network of commercial connections especially in Europe and India. Their fleets controlled the eastern Mediterranean and they gradually extended their rule down both shores of the Red Sea. Commercial bankers used promissory notes and offered loans with interest; traders sold on credit and payment could be made in instalment. In the bazaars of the twin cities of Cairo and al-Fustat produce and wares from Alexandria, Basra, Yemen, Baghdad, Armenia, Abyssinia, China, India, Muscat, Ceylon, Spain, Tunisia and the Baltic were available.

During the eleventh and twelth centuries, repeated attempts were made by Christian Crusader armies to reclaim the Holy Land from Islamic rule. The Fatimid caliphs of Egypt did not consistently oppose the Crusaders, but in AD 117 Salah ad-Din (Saladin) re-established normal rule from Baghdad, and became the first **Ayyubid** to rule the country. Although Salah al Din built the citadel, which overlooks the city of Cairo, he spent most of the time fighting the Crusaders in the region. The Ayyubid dynasty came to a violent end with the murder of the female sultan, Shagar al-Durr.

Saladin

The **Mamluke** era inaugurated by Beybars the Crossbowman lasted from 1250 to 1517. During this period Egypt again became dominant in the region. The Mamlukes – a caste of soldier-slaves – established commercial treaties with Ceylon, Venice, Florence and Genoa, and amassed huge wealth from the trade in eastern spices. However, Egyptian trade was dealt a serious blow when Vasco da Gama discovered the Cape of Good Hope route around Africa (1497), considerably reducing Egypt's income from the spice trade.

In 1517 the **Ottoman Turks** conquered the country, although the Mamlukes retained considerable autonomy and Cairo remained an important commercial centre. In 1798 Napoleon landed in Alexandria intending to disrupt British commerce with India, routed the Mamlukes at Imbaba and occupied Cairo. However, Nelson destroyed his fleet at the Battle of the Nile and, abandoning his army, Napoleon returned to France. The French were swiftly defeated by a combined Ottoman–British invasion.

The Ottomans

1

Mohammad Ali

One of the most significant figures in recent Egyptian history was **Mohammad Ali** (ruled 1805–1849). Appointed viceroy by the Ottomans, he destroyed the last vestiges of Mamluke power. Inviting their remaining leaders for a feast at the citadel, he slaughtered all 500 of them. In theory Mohammad Ali was a servant of the Ottoman sultan, however, his control over Egypt was absolute. He confiscated lands and with European help built railways, factories and irrigation canals. He also introduced cotton to Egypt, which subsequently became a major source of income.

Completed in 1869 by the **Khedive Ismail** (1863–1879), the Suez Canal was to become another major source of revenue for Egypt, and it remains so today. Ismail was an ambitious and progressive ruler, expanding the railway network and improving irrigation canals. He created a parliament, completed the transition from Islamic to Napoleonic law and welcomed immigrants, even allowing them to own land. He abolished slavery – albeit half-heartedly – but taxed the peasants cruelly.

Modernisation

Ismail modernised Cairo at vast expense with the assistance of European banks and financiers. By 1875 Egypt's debt to foreign bankers stood at £100m, equivalent to ten years of cotton revenue, and the Khedive had to sell off the country's assets, including its share in the Suez Canal to the British for £4m, to service these debts. Ismail went into exile in 1879 leaving the throne to his son **Tewfik** who again relied heavily on British and French support. In 1881 a group of Egyptian nationalist army officers, led by Ahmed Arabi, revolted against Tewfik. The British intervened, the nationalists were defeated and Tewfik was restored as ruler under British control. Although nominally independent, in practice Egypt was a British colony, ruled by British officials, exporting its cotton to England, which had been bought from the farmers at artificially low prices. Any manufactured goods wanted by Egypt were imported from Britain.

World War I

The next major event in the country's history was World War I. In 1914, Egypt was still nominally a part of the Ottoman Empire which had sided with Germany against the British. In November of that year, Britain therefore declared Egypt a protectorate, a status which the country retained until 1922 when independence under **Fouad**, the sixth son of Ismail, was granted. The British retained control of the Canal, the legal system, defence and communications. In 1936 **Farouk,** Fouad's son, signed an Anglo-Egyptian treaty which ended British occupation but gave them the authority to maintain troops on the canal.

During the Second World War, Egypt became one of the allies' main strategic assets. The government of the nationalist Wafd party agreed to suspend their ambitions for full independence until after the war, in order to keep local tensions under control. Cairo became a centre of international intrigue and a home for exiled royalty from the Balkan states. The fortunes of British army fighting in the Western Desert fluctuated wildly, with Italian forces occupying Siwa oasis to the west of Cairo, and Rommel's Afrika Korps coming within a few miles of Alexandria. In 1942 at El Alamein, General Montgomery turned the tide of the war in north Africa and British control of Egypt was not threatened again until after 1945.

World War II

The French

The brief French occupation left an indelible mark on Egypt and its society: the Napoleonic legal system was introduced and remains today the basis for Egyptian law; the French language became the language of society and the ruling classes. Treasures gathered by the French, including the Rosetta Stone which had been discovered by a French army officer at Rosetta in the delta, were appropriated by the British. The Rosetta Stone, the key to ancient Egyptian hieroglyphic inscriptions, resides in the British Museum rather than the Louvre in France.

1

After the war, nationalism and resentment of British interference culminated in the military coup of 1952 and the forced abdication and exile of King Farouk. Although General Naquib, the senior officer was ostensibly in control of the country, the power behind him was the Revolutionary Command Council, which included **Gamal Abdul Nasser** and on 26th July 1953 Egypt was declared a republic. In 1954 Nasser became premier, deposed Naguib and, two years later, officially assumed the office of president.

The Revolution

The Suez crisis

In 1954 Nasser had reached agreement with the British for them to withdraw their troops from the **Suez Canal**, while control of the canal remained with the foreign company. However, by 1956, as a result of losing US finance for the Aswan high dam – itself a result of Egypt's acceptance of Soviet arms – Nasser was in desperate need of money. He therefore nationalised the canal. Israel invaded Sinai, while Anglo-French forces bombarded Port Said and landed paratroops along the canal. Widespread opposition in Britain and France plus pressure from the Soviet Union and the United States produced a rapid withdrawal and Nasser scored a notable political victory. The Suez crisis was over with the canal reopening under full Egyptian control.

The Napoleonic Code

The coup in 1952 transformed the country and introduced socialism. Land was expropriated from landowners and distributed to the peasants, the *fellaheen*. As the years passed, the Egyptian inheritance laws, based on the Napoleonic Code, led to further fragmentation of holdings until today some farms are so small they are not sufficient to support more than one small family. In 1952, land rents were frozen, a state of affairs which persisted until 1998 when reforms re-introduced the free market into land tenure.

Also in 1952, house rents were frozen, so that from generation to generation property rents have failed to increase. Landlords receive insufficient revenue from their tenants to pay for the upkeep of the property. The owner of one block of flats in the most expensive area of Zamalek, central Cairo, does not receive enough rent from all his apartments to pay for the monthly salary of the watchman, the *boab*.

Nasser now dominated Egypt and the Middle East with his blend of Arab nationalism and socialism. He formed a short-lived United Arab Republic with Syria in 1958 and supported a revolutionary movement in Yemen with advisors and combat forces. He also became a significant international figure in the nonalignment movement alongside such leaders as Tito and Nehru.

1

In 1967 the **Six-Day War** resulted in a catastrophic defeat for Egypt with Israel occupying the whole of Sinai, and even briefly crossing the canal. However, such was Nasser's prestige that he survived even this setback, and his death in 1970 was a shock to the whole country. Millions of Egyptians turned out for the funeral even threatening the Kasr el-Nil bridge over the Nile with collapse.

The new president was **Anwar Sadat**, later principally remembered for his major peace achievements in the region, but also leader during the next war against Israel. On 6th October 1973, Egyptian forces stormed the Israeli positions on the canal and retook some of western Sinai. While they did not maintain control of all their gains for long, they did however remain on the east bank of the canal. Egypt's pride had been restored.

After the war an amnesty was granted to political prisoners, press censorship was eased and political parties, including the Muslim Brotherhood, were allowed. Sadat also developed his 'open door' policy, allowing foreign investment in the country and reducing government involvement in the economy. The oil-rich Gulf Arabs were big investors and although the economic boom created a number of millionaires and fuelled the expansion of the middle class, the urban poor and country peasants failed to benefit. Half-hearted attempts at reform and privatisation were not encouraged by high oil prices.

In 1979, following the US-brokered **Camp David** agreement, the Israelis agreed to withdraw from the remainder of Sinai, and Egypt recognised Israel's right to exist. The recognition of Israel outraged Arab opinion and prompted the Arab League council to withdraw their ambassadors from Cairo, withdraw their investments, reduce political and economic links and move the Arab League headquarters from Cairo to Tunis. In order to support the weakened Egyptian economy American investment was established at about $2bn per annum. These funds were – and continue to be – vital to the country's finances, but the rise in foreign, non-Arab, involvement in Egypt resulted in the emergence of Islamic militants, culminating in 1981 in the assassination of President Sadat.

His successor, **Hosni Mubarak** continued the peace process and Israel completed its withdrawal from Sinai in 1982. Two years later, Mubarak's party was elected in

War with Israel

Peace with Israel

1

27

the first multi party elections and in 1987 Mubarak was re-elected president of Egypt; an achievement repeated in 1993. The early years of his presidency were troubled with massive foreign debt and with the continued rise of Islamic fundamentalism. The *Achille Lauro* affair and the hijacking of an Egyptair flight from Rome caused international concern and a decline in tourism revenue, while the police riots in 1986 resulted in a crackdown on terrorism and fundamentalists.

Mubarak also focused his attention on the problems of Cairo and its crumbling infrastructure: new flyovers were constructed to ease the congestion caused by a million cars on roads designed for half that amount. American and British companies started renewing the sewers of the capital and other cities; France began a metro line; Japan supplied an opera house (to replace the one destroyed by fire in 1970) and China donated an exhibition and conference centre. By the end of the 1980s nearly 75 per cent of households in Cairo had running water and dwellings with electricity had doubled from one third at the beginning of the decade to more than two thirds by the end.

Probably the turning point in Egypt's economy was the **Gulf War** in 1992 when Egypt supported the West against Iraq. As a result of this support the West cancelled significant outstanding debts. Meanwhile, the annual US aid given to Egypt as a result of the Camp David agreement continued, tourism boomed, canal revenues were very healthy and Egyptian expatriates in the Gulf and Saudi Arabia continued to remit significant amounts of money.

Egypt Today

Today Egypt is gravitating towards the West. It has become a model form of an emerging market and an example of the effect of the policies of the International Monetary Fund – although in the recent past the relationship has not been good. Inflation is below 4 per cent, sustained growth is more than 5 per cent, budget deficit is about 1 per cent of GDP and foreign reserves are currently just under $16bn. Exchange controls have been abolished, bureaucracy is being eased and information about the economic state of the country is available.

Although large state organisations and nationalised industries continued to operate, modern industrial and business practices are prevailing. Publicly owned companies are increasingly being taken over by the private sector. The Egyptian stock exchange flourishes and has ambitions to return to being one of the five largest in the world.

The Muslim Brotherhood and Islamic fundamentalism

The rise of Islam as a political force in modern Egypt can be traced back to 1928 when the Muslim Brotherhood was founded in Ismailia. The brotherhood advocated a revival of Islamic codes of morality and established schools, training centres and secret paramilitary groups. At the end of the Second World War, the brotherhood had spread throughout Egypt and the Middle East and in 1949 King Farouk banned the organisation, forcing it underground. In 1954, after two years of revival following Egyptian independence, the Brotherhood had become disillusioned with the government and tried to assassinate Nasser. The organisation was again banned and did not reappear in Egypt until the Sadat era, when it was encouraged as a counterweight to the left. By then the mainstream Brotherhood had become more moderate. However, fundamentalist factions broke away, including various groups generally known as Islamic Jihad, notably al-Jihad who were responsible for the death of Sadat. In the early 1990s with the rise of fundamentalism in Algeria, the Egyptian government cracked down on the fundamentalists with massive arrests. Rules for unions and professional associations were changed so that Islamic groups lost their control of these organisations. The current group troubling the government with its acts of terrorism carried out in the name of Islam is the *Gamaat Islamia*, which was responsible for the Luxor incident and other acts of.violence against tourists.

The country's infrastructure is being systematically upgraded. Build Operate Own and Transfer (BOOT) power stations, water projects, airports and roads are being developed by private companies. New industrial and commercial cities continue to grow, and are seen as increasingly desirable places to live by the Egyptian middle classes. Major irrigation schemes have been started to reclaim areas of desert for agriculture, habitation and industry. The coastal areas of Egypt on the Mediterranean, the Red Sea and the Gulf of Aqaba are major tourist resorts for international and local holidaymakers.

The New Rich

During the austere years of the Nasser era, those fortunate enough to have money were reluctant to display their wealth: apartment block entrances were gloomy and gave no hint of the luxury hidden behind the individual front doors; only modest family cars were seen on the streets. Things are now very different: ostentatious apartments are being built; expensive imported cars are everywhere, and new boutiques displaying the latest from America and Europe are opening every day. Smart restaurants are full of chic diners gossiping into their new mobile phones. For the really affluent the prospect of flying off in their private jet to their seaside villa, for a round or two of golf on one of the many new courses on the 'Med' or in Sinai, is now a real possibility.

Egypt has a long way to go before this kind of affluence and luxury is available to more than a tiny minority. Government still has many radical changes to make to the legal system, and the poorly paid civil service, currently contracting due to early retirement and low recruitment, needs to be further streamlined. Democracy is still limited with many key appointments being made by the president. The majority of people, unable to afford the expensive facilities offered by the private schools and hospitals, only have recourse to the basic services of the State institutions.

1

investigating the potential market

investigating the potential market

2

An outline of some of the myriad organisations which exist to assist the exporter, along with an assessment of their focus and likely relevance.

Sources of Information

The business traveller should be as well informed as possible before entering a new market. This section is a guide for such information. It includes government and private sources in electronic and hardcopy format and discusses the availability of reliable market and economic information.

Whether you are visiting Egypt for the first time or making the latest in a series of visits, preparation is essential to get the most out of the trip and ensure your project succeeds. Obtaining the latest information will allow you to plan effectively for your trip, get a clear picture of the market you are entering, identify any trends or opportunities that you can use to your advantage and spot any possible pitfalls. It is equally important to ensure the information you use is accurate and that you are aware of any possible bias.

However, do not expect to gain an instant understanding of the market or instant results. The sources below can provide a starting point for research on the Egyptian market. Many are free or provide information at very little cost. The information thus gained will provide a good overview of the market.

2

Egyptian Embassies

US

Embassy of the Arab Republic of Egypt
3521 International Court, NW.
Washington, DC 20008
❑ Tel: (202) 895-5400; fax: (202) 244 4319/2445131
(202) 966 6342 (Consular Section)

In addition to the embassy, Egypt also has a number of other important offices in the diplomatic capital.

Office of Commercial and Economic Affairs
2232 Massachusetts Ave. NW,
Washington, DC, 20008
❑ Tel: (202) 265 9111; fax: (202) 328 4517

Office of Cultural and Educational Affairs
1303 New Hampshire Ave, NW
Washington, DC, 20036
❑ Tel: (202) 296 3888; fax: (202) 296 3891

US

33

Office of the Defense and Military Attache
2308 Tracy Pl, NW
Washington, DC, 20008
❑ Tel: (202) 462 5943; fax: (202) 462 5978

Office of Procurement
5500 16th St, NW
Washington, DC, 20011
❑ Tel: (202) 726 8006; fax: (202) 829 4909

Office of Press and Information
1666 Connecticut Ave, 4th Fl, NW
Washington, DC, 20009
❑ Tel: (202) 667 3402; fax: (202) 234 6827

Office of Medical Affairs
3521 International Court, NW
Washington, DC, 20008
❑ Tel: (202) 296 5286; fax: (202) 296 5288

Office of Agricultural Affairs
3521 International Court, NW
Washington, DC, 20008
❑ Tel: (202) 966 2080; fax: (202) 895 5493

Email: [EgyptEmbassy@USA.net]
Much of the information you may need can be accessed
via the Embassy's website: [www.Egyptianembassy.net].

UK
Egyptian Embassy
26 South Street
London, W1Y 6DD
❑ Tel: (020) 7499 2401/(020) 7499 3304

Australia
Australian High Commission
Strand
London, WC2B 4LA
❑ Tel: (020) 7379 4334; fax: (020) 7240 5333

US Ministries and other Government Agencies

The main official United States source for information on
overseas markets is the US Commercial Service, under the
Department of Commerce's Trade Information Center.
The US Commercial Service offers trade counseling and

contacts, promotes US companies, researches markets, acts as an advocate to US businesses, provides information on financing, and checks the credit of possible overseas business partners, among other services.

Trade Information Center, International Trade Administration
US Department of Commerce
Washington, DC 20230
❑ Tel: 1 800 USA TRADE; fax: 202 482 4473
Email: [TIC@ita.doc.gov]

Its website contains a directory of trade contacts at the federal, state and local levels for US exporters. The directory can be viewed by state, division and zip code.
Website: [www.ita.doc.gov/TICFrameset.html].

Commercial Support for US Companies

Specific Information and Support

The specific start point for any US company wishing to consider doing business in Egypt would be to approach their local US Export Assistance Center of the International Trade Administration, US and Foreign Commercial Service of the US Department of Commerce. (*See* Appendix 3.)

Military Sales

The Bureau of Export Administration's Office of Strategic Industries and Economic Security provides defence market research, analysis and technology reports, business opportunities, and advocacy assistance for foreign military sales.

US Department of Commerce
Room 3876 BXA
14th and Constitution Ave. N.W.
Washington, DC 20230
❑ Tel: (202) 482 4060
Website: [www.bxa.doc.gov/OSIES/]

Other US Ministries

The US State Department and the Department of Commerce provide a wide range of information to US companies or representatives of US companies operating in Egypt.

US

2

The Country Commercial Guide, obtained for a fee from the US State Department, offers a comprehensive look at the business environment.

To order:

❏ Tel: 1 800 STATUSA
Website: [www.stat-usa.gov]

Government Acronyms

The DTI, like most government offices around the world, uses acronyms wherever possible. Indeed when an acronym cannot be concocted the use of initial letters for departments is used – even when it may take longer to say or use! So it is that the DTI offers services like the late BOTB (British Overseas Trade Board), JEPD (couldn't make an acronym from this), EMIC (easy to say), PEP (no relation to the investments), GONE (which is not self-explanatory), OSO (can be viewed in any direction and upside down) and X triple A. There is BREEZE (British Exclusive Economic Zone Export Team), IPPA (Investment Promotion and Protection Agreements), BNSC (British National Space Centre – suitably housed in a small but smart establishment in Eccleston Square, quite unlike its equivalent in the United States) and NPL CQM (the National Physical Laboratory Centre for Quantum Metrology – a very popular venue) – to name but a few. And then spare a thought for that senior mandarin the Parliamentary Under-Secretary of State (PUSS). And somewhere within the organisation has to be a group inventing acronyms and names. For, while the functions of these offices generally remain, their locations and names, like the officials in them, are changing continually. And when there are no major institutional changes to be made, the furniture removal men will move offices and their contents from one floor to another within the building over a weekend – just to keep in practice. While this might be difficult for DTI visitors it's even worse for those whose desks are on the move and those who are required to keep the internal telephone directory up to date.

2

Official UK Sources of Information

UK

In London the primary sources are the British government's Department of Trade and Industry (DTI), Foreign and Commonwealth Office (FCO), and other specialist departments, including the Department for the Environment, Transport and the Regions (DETR). The DETR is the government authority currently responsible for the construction industry, transport and aviation. Other departments deal with areas such as health, defence, agriculture and will have specialists concerned with exports.

The DTI and FCO are probably the most important UK government sources of information and advice and have formed a joint venture which currently operates as **Trade Partners UK** (formerly British Trade International, and before that Overseas Trade Services).

UK Regional Offices

Other sources include the London embassies of the United States and the Arab Republic of Egypt, the various offices of the European Union and non-governmental bodies such as trade associations and chambers of commerce.

2

The Department of Trade and Industry

The head office of the DTI is in Victoria Street London. Halfway between Victoria Station and the Palace of Westminster is Kingsgate House, 66–74 Victoria Street, where the export desks for all countries are based. Other DTI offices include 1, Victoria Street, where the principal executives, including the Secretary of State, have their offices.

DTI

Your first task is to contact the DTI desk officer for Egypt who will know whom to contact within the UK government system for the best advice. Start here and persevere! Ask questions about sources of further information. What is the competition? Is there a market for the product or service? Are there any restrictions on export from the UK or problems importing the product into Egypt? Who else can give particular advice? Is there any published information available from the DTI? (There is.) Can he or she suggest any contacts in Egypt? While they may not know all the answers they will know someone who does.

❏ DTI: +44 20 7215 4947 or by e-mail on [exportinfo.nafrica@eirv.dti.gov.uk].

UK

One of the most useful sources of primary information at the DTI is the **Export Market Information Centre** (EMIC) – currently known as DTI XP7. EMIC has a comprehensive library of information – statistics, trade directories, development plans, telephone directories (Yellow Pages where they exist), company profiles and catalogues. This information is available as hard copy and CD ROM. EMIC can be found on the Internet at [www.dti.uk/ots/emic]. Access to the library is free and

EMIC

books and guides on Egypt are available in the bookshop. In addition to the library, EMIC can carry out fee-based research in association with the British Embassy.

❑ EMIC: +44 20 7215 5444/4351 or by e-mail at [EMIC@xpd3.dti.gov.uk].

Internet information is also available for those exporting companies that register with the DTI's export service Database. This service is currently free and offers overseas buyers the opportunity to contact a UK company directly. Look in [www.tradeuk.com] for information or contact the service through [export@dialog.com]. In addition to this British DTI service, Egypt has its own source of Internet information. [www.connectegypt.co.uk] is a page recently set up to provide information, leads in Egypt and details of local contacts.

PEP

Projects Export Division (PEP) is the next port of call for a would-be exporter to Egypt. This department is responsible for major exports and overseas projects including railways, airports and power plants. PEP also deals with project finance and world aid programmes. Information about proposed and existing projects is available on a regular basis, fed to PEP's World Aid Section (WAS) directly from the source of aid: the European Union, World Bank, African Development Bank, etc.

For those unable to visit London there are regional and local offices offering similar services: for example the Government Office for the North East (GONE) in Newcastle. There are nine other GO locations, and Business Link offices are in most major towns in the UK, often situated in or near the local chamber of commerce. Organisations like the Northern Development Company, which was set up in a region for the specific purpose of assisting the unemployed, will have an individual or even

2

a team with experience in exporting products worldwide. They may offer direct assistance to develop an overseas market using specialist consultants who will work alongside the company's team.

Scottish Trade International in Glasgow are very active in Egypt, and their local officer will be familiar with Egypt and in particular the investment opportunities.

The Oil and Gas Projects Supplies Office (OSO), with offices in London, Glasgow and Aberdeen, not only supports the industries in the North Sea but assists companies to export their technology and equipment.

Another source of assistance, totally free, are the **Export Promoters** (EPs) who are business people seconded to the DTI from British industry for a period of up to three years. The majority of these experts have specialised knowledge of particular countries; a few are industry specialists. Some countries, like Egypt where great potential for trade is recognised by the DTI, may have more than one promoter. EPs can be contacted by anyone. They are likely to be frequent visitors to their countries of responsibility and will have a lot of information relating to opportunities, agents, partners, exhibitions, trade missions, etc. They can generally be found through the country desk officer at the DTI Kingsgate House. EPs are expected to be well informed and should give direct, unbiased answers about their markets and whether an opportunity for a particular company might exist. Their time and assistance is free and they will usually be able to help a company with introductions and contacts at the highest level – they report directly to the minister for trade in the UK and work closely with the commercial section of the British Embassy in their country of responsibility.

ECGD or the **Export Credits Guarantee Department**, is also associated with the DTI, but is financially self-supporting. The services offered by this organisation are very specialised and complex but, essentially, it operates a scheme to insure overseas investments made by British business organisations. It is an arguable point that if ECGD cover is available then the risk involved is minimal and that it might be better to save the premiums. ECGD can, however, offer some methods for a prospective client to defer payments to an exporter. This facility can have its attractions.

2

ECGD

One of the most common ways in which ECGD becomes involved with an export opportunity is through a line of credit. When a UK bank offers a facility to an overseas bank to enable goods or services to be purchased from the UK, ECGD can insure that risk. The loan facility is used to pay the exporter once the goods have been exported or the service performed. If the borrower fails to repay any part of the loan then the UK bank is covered by the ECGD guarantee. Overseas investment insurance is also available.

❑ ECGD: +44 20 7512 7000 or by e-mail on [help@ecgd.gov.uk]; or visit their web page [www.open.gov.uk/ecgd]

Foreign and Commonwealth Office

FCO

The FCO, situated off Whitehall in London, also has desk officers who are concerned with particular countries. In London they are not so involved with commercial affairs, but can advise business people about the political situation within an area. The FCO and the commercial section of the British Embassy in Cairo will have their own view of the needs of Egypt, and the expertise that the UK may have to offer. However, Egypt can accommodate most commercial opportunities. The FCO also has information available via the Internet on [www.fco.gov.uk]. This page also gives travel advice for Egypt – particularly important in periods of unrest or international tension.

❑ British Embassy: +202 794 0850 or by e-mail on [britemb@idsc.gov.eg]. Web page [www.britishembassy.org.eg].

Department of Environment, Transport and the Regions

DETR

In recent years, the DETR have taken a particular interest in Egypt. In 1997 and again in 1998 senior officials visited Egypt together with business people who were particularly interested in construction and environmental issues – lawyers, bankers, contractors, town planners, consultants and manufacturers – all either hoping to break into the market or aiming to consolidate existing activities. The DETR is very active in promoting its services and UK businesses throughout the world, and

2

has been particularly active in the Middle East and Egypt.

❏ DETR: +44 20 7890 3000 or by e-mail on [www.detr.gov.uk]

Military Sales

Advice on sales of military equipment can be obtained from a specialist organisation in London, the **Defence Export Sales Organisation** (DESO), part of the Ministry of Defence. This is a very active export service manned by senior diplomats on temporary secondment to DESO. The business is very specialised and overseas is not handled by the embassy commercial offices but by the defence attachés. Defence sales include obvious military hardware and equipment but also takes in the construction of airfields, supply of 4x4 vehicles and uniforms, etc. DESO will also advise on any relevant political sensitivities.

DESO

Education

The UK Ministry of Education does not take an active part in promoting the export capabilities of its associated industries; this task is undertaken by the **British Council**. The Council is responsible for promoting British culture overseas and is very active in supporting UK educational and cultural enterprises. The Council, with offices in London and Manchester and throughout the UK, is financially self-supporting and has therefore, perhaps reluctantly at first, entered the world of commerce. It has officers responsible for exports and for liaison with other government bodies, in particular the DTI.

❏ British Council: +44 20 7389 4141, or visit their web page [www.britcoun.org.] or [www.britishcouncil.org.eg].

Other British Ministries

Two other ministries which promote UK exports are the departments of agriculture and health. The export departments in these ministries have specialised sector information freely available to any business people. Overseas visits by ministers and officials accompanied by business people are frequently arranged.

❏ Ministry of Health: [www.gov.uk]
❏ Ministry of Agriculture: [www.maff.gov.uk]

2

In general, all UK government offices can be found on [www.open.gov.uk].

Support from the European Union

The most relevant office of the European Union (EU) is Directorate General 1 (DG1), which deals with trade and political matters; it is based in Brussels and has overseas representative offices. DG1 controls the Mediterranean Development Aid (MEDA) programme, a substantial sum of aid and loans (currently 11bn Euros) available for selected projects in the region including Egypt. DG1 also controls the **European Community Investment Partners** scheme (ECIP), and relations with the **European Investment Bank** (EIB). DG1 has country desks, much the same as the British DTI and the FCO, with desk officers, who can offer information and assistance.

There are funds available from the union for various development programmes apart from direct project finance, including money for companies to set up partnerships and/or joint ventures in Egypt. The ECIP scheme can assist with finance to form such a joint venture and with training of personnel. ECIP can also finance feasibility studies prior to a joint venture agreement.

Further assistance and advice can be obtained from the commercial section of the United Kingdom Permanent Representation (UKRep) office in Brussels, which exists to assist British companies to understand and participate in the programmes administered by the European Union. EMIC at the DTI in London can also help and a Development Business Team in the DTI's Export Promotion Directorate assists small and medium sized enterprises (SMEs) to win business connected with aid funded projects. Registration with Brussels for consultants is essential. Manufacturers with specialised products should also get pre-qualified to participate in EU funded projects.

Australia

Austrade

The Australian Trade Commission or Austrade, is the federal governments export and investment facilitation agency. Austrade provides advice to Australian companies on general export issues, assistance in determining which overseas markets hold potential for their products and aid in building a presence in the market. Through their network of global offices, including one in Riyadh, Austrade can assist with finding potential business partners or agents, prepare publicity material, organise product launches and offer assistance with attending suitable exhibitions. If Austrade cannot help with your specific requirement, they will direct you to an appropriate government or private service which can.

Austrade Online is an enhanced website facility at [www.austrade.gov.au] which provides up-to-date reference points regarding international trade issues and export programmes. Australian companies can also take out a free of charge listing within the website allowing inclusion on a searchable database of products and services.

Under their **Export Market Development Grant** (EMDG) scheme, Austrade may be able to reimburse eligible businesses for part of the export marketing costs they incur.

Further Sources of Information Internationally

This is not a definitive list of bodies and merely indicates the types of organisations that exist and how they might help.

The Middle East Association

The Middle East Association is an independent private organisation set up in 1961 by a number of British companies to promote trade between the UK and the Middle East. It is non-political and non-profit making and is financed entirely by private subscription. It works with Middle Eastern embassies in London and with other official and semi official bodies including the FCO, the DTI, the ECGD, COMET and the Confederation of British Industry (CBI). It also liaises with trade associations and chambers of commerce in the UK and overseas. The aim of the association is to offer its members advice on all aspects of Middle East trade and to channel to them business opportunities, introductions and enquiries from overseas. The Association has a library and information centre at its offices in Bury Street – offices it shares with COMET. With the support of the DTI it sponsors overseas missions and UK participation in trade exhibitions in the Middle East. The association holds regular functions at its headquarters for its members and a fortnightly information digest is circulated to its members.

❑ MEA: +44 20 7839 2137 or visit their web page on [www.the-mea.co.uk].

The Egyptian-British Chamber of Commerce

The Egyptian-British Chamber of Commerce was set up in 1979, taking over the Egyptian responsibilities of the more broadly-based Arab-British Chamber of Commerce. These include certification of export licenses required by any companies shipping goods to Egypt. The chamber has links with Egyptian-British trade groups in Cairo. At their offices in the centre of London, the chamber has general and trade directories for Egypt available to personal callers and also publishes regular bulletins on business opportunities together with commentaries on recent events in Egypt.

❑ EBCC: +44 20 7499 3100.

The Arab-British Chambers of Commerce

The Arab-British Chamber of Commerce (ABCC) was founded in 1975 and represents all the Arab chambers of commerce and the main UK Chambers. Similar in its activities to the Egyptian British Chamber, the ABCC is responsible for trade and economic interests matters throughout the Middle East with the exception of Egypt. A regular journal is published. The ABCC is also a facilitator for the European Community Investment Partners scheme (ECIP) and has details of how to access the programme, together with information about many of the other EU funding programmes. Although not directly involved with Egypt, it does however have access to useful information and personal contacts there.

❑ ABBC :+44 20 7235 4363 or by e-mail on [bims@abccbims.force9.co.uk].

Trade Associations

There is a trade association for every conceivable industry in the UK – even the Briar Pipe Trade Association. Some are large and particularly active in promoting exports. These organisations will assist their members to take part in trade fairs, can organise seminars and conferences to run concurrently with these events and may target particular countries where they believe the greatest

2

Feel at home

with Click GSM

No matter how far you are from home and regardless where exactly do you plan to go in Egypt, Click GSM will be covering you, to keep you connected to your home country, and the world.

Click GSM is a part of Vodafone Group

Roam with Click GSM*

You can rely on us

Click GSM..

A world of reliability

Click GSM has firmly established itself as the leading telecommunications company in Egypt.

In less than 2 years of operations, Click GSM has:

- created a wide range of flexible pricing schemes that suits everyone.
- always been the leader in covering all the governorates of Egypt as well as the major highways.
- always been the leader in introducing the latest mobile technology to Egypt. e.g. SMS, W@P, fax & data, IVR & conference call.
- had roaming agreements with most of the GSM networks in more than 75 countries.
- maintained superior network quality, thus...
  proved to be the reliable gsm network of Egypt.

You can rely on us

opportunities exist for their members.

Full details of all British associations are available from CBD Research Ltd in Kent, who publish a directory in hard copy or CD-ROM format. CBD can be found on the Internet on [www.glen.co.uk]. In addition, addresses and contacts at these associations can be found through the DTI. Many associations are developing their own websites.

Export clubs also exist. These are informal local groups that meet occasionally to exchange experiences and ideas and to assist each other to develop their businesses.

Seminars and conferences are a good place to meet others associated with Egypt or a particular industry. The content of the presentations at such gatherings and the opportunity for networking during the intervals are both important. The Middle East Association holds a monthly 'at home' where members meet and discuss the current issues and opportunities in the area, including Egypt.

Publications such as the *Middle East Economic Digest* (MEED), the *Economist* and the *Economist Intelligence Unit Country Report for Egypt*, provide useful background reading.

2

Digging Deeper

Once you have an overview of the market in the United Arab Emirates, you may want more detailed economic information or wish to concentrate on your particular sector. This is where the cost of research starts to increase – but you will be very well informed and the risk of unpleasant surprises later on will be much reduced. You will be aware of the trends and the possible effects on your business and therefore able to plan for them.

Economic and Country guides

Two of the best sources of detailed economic information and analysis are **Dun & Bradstreet** (D&B) and the **Economist Intelligence Unit** (EIU). D&B offer an authoratative web-based information service which includes data on Egypt. The D&B Country Risk Service delivers comprehensive information sources for evaluating risk and opportunities. Their approach is to combine constant monitoring with an archive service on a wide range of topics. Most companies can qualify for a 14-day free trial period. D&B also offer two excellent

D&B

business support publications. The first is the *Exporters' Encyclopaedia* – an annual publication that provides information and advice on exporting to almost every country in the world. The second is the *International Risk and Payment Review* – a monthly publication that allows companies to keep up-to-date on issues affecting the local trading environment.

Dun & Bradstreet
899 Eaton Avenue
Bethlehem
PA 18025
USA
❑ Tel: +44 1-800 932 0025; fax +44 1 610 882 6005

Or

Dun & Bradstreet
Holmer's Farm Way
High Wycombe
Bucks, HP12 4UL
❑ Tel: +44 1494 422000; fax: +44 1494 422260
Website: [www.dunandbrad.co.uk]

The Economist Intelligence Unit produces a range of quarterly and annual publications which provide a detailed political and economic analysis of Egypt. They offer a *Country Report*, an up-to-date monitoring information service, *Country Profile*, which combines historical data and background with current reportage, and a forecast service entitled the *Country Risk Service*.

The Economist Building
111 West 57th Street
New York, NY 10019
USA
❑ Tel: +44 1-212 554 0600; fax: +44 1 212 586 1181

Or

EIU
15 Regent Street
London, SW1Y 4LR
❑ Tel: +44 20 7830 1000; fax: +44 20 7830 1023
Website: [www.eiu.com]; e-mail: [london@eiu.com]

Another valuable source of information is the **Middle East Economic Digest** (MEED) who publish a number of country reports and financial profiles, including the

Middle East Business Finance Directory of the top 500 companies in the region. MEED also offers a CD-ROM offering archive material going back five years. The *Middle East Economic Digest* itself, though perhaps a rather dry read, is, nevertheless mandatory reading for anyone who wants to keep abreast of commercial, economic and political issues in the region. MEED has a first class team of writers based in the region.

MEED

MEED
21 John Street
London WC1N 2BP
❏ Tel: +44 20 7505 8000; fax: +44 20 7831 9537
Website: [www.meed.com]

Banks, particularly the larger institutions that operate across the globe, are also a useful source of information. This can usually be accessed through the banks' websites.

Another useful source of market information and news/archive material is **Reuters Business Briefing** – a CD ROM or web-based information service allowing subscribers to search a vast range of information sources for material on virtually any subject matter. It is particularly good at digesting and reproducing news flows from the Middle East and is a good way of following trends as well as tracking down information on individual companies.

Dow Jones Reuters Business Briefing
Reuters Limited
85 Fleet Street
London, EC4P 4AJ
❏ Tel: +44 207 5425043

Also worth bearing in mind are the trade associations – there is one for almost every conceivable industry. Some of these are large and active in promoting exports. They will assist their members to take part in trade fairs, can organise seminars and conferences to run concurrently with these events and may target particular countries where they believe the greatest opportunities exist for their members. Those which have been particularly active in the United Arab Emirates include:

British Footwear Association
❏ Tel: +44 20 7580 8687

British Contract Furnishing Association
❏ Tel: +44 20 7226 6641

Computing Services and Software Association
❏ Tel: +44 1325 340072

Environmental Industries Commission
❏ Tel: +44 20 7935 1670

Telecommunications Industry Association
❏ Tel: +44 1908 645000

Full lists of all the associations in the UK are available from **CBD Research Ltd** in Kent, who publish a directory in hard copy or in CD-ROM format – full details at [www.glen.co.uk]. Further information is also available from Trade Partners UK.

Seminars and conferences are a good place to meet others associated with Egypt or with a particular industry. The content of the presentations at such gatherings and the opportunities for networking during the intervals are both important. The Middle East Association holds a monthly 'at home' where members meet and discuss the different issues and opportunities in the area.

Travel advice

The most convenient source of travel advice from the UK is the **Foreign and Commonwealth Office** (FCO) travel advisory service. This can be accessed either by telephone or on-line. It provides succinct information and advice on natural disasters, health concerns, security and political issues. It is more than adequate for most business travellers' needs. Be aware though that it is aimed at a wide audience and is not geared solely towards the business visitor's requirements.

The FCO travel advisory service can be contacted on:

❏ Tel: +44 20 7238 4503/4
Website: [www.fco.gov.uk/travel]

Or on Ceefax on BBC2 page 470

The US State Department advice service can be found at: [www.state.gov/travel_warnings]. Their reports can sometimes seem alarmist as they are legally obliged to publish any threats to US citizens and their property of which it is aware. Also see [www.usis.egnet.net]

FCO

2

For travel information and advice geared specifically towards the business traveller's needs, you must turn to the private sector. Here there are some good but expensive services which provide more frequently updated reports than the FCO or State Department travel notices. These services tend to be more forward-looking, commenting for instance on the likelihood of further security incidents or the possible deterioration or improvement in the travel environment. They are also usually more frank about a country as they do not have the same political restraints as the FCO or State Department.

Keeping up to date

Publications

After you have thoroughly researched the Egypt market and started operations in the country, it is essential to keep up-to-date about developments both in your particular sector and in the wider market.

The easiest way is to monitor the press and media for stories on Egypt. The country receives adequate coverage in the international press and most British newspapers and news organisations have correspondents based in the region. The internet editions of some newspapers and media organisations offer news e-mail services, which send stories on specified subjects to your e-mail address.

Others allow you to produce customised pages, which are updated with stories on your chosen subjects. One of the best is CNN's service (see [cnn.com]).

The Internet

Publications

Business Today Egypt – local monthly business magazine [www.businesstoday-eg.com].

Egypt Today – general monthly source of information about Egypt, hotels, restaurants, what's on etc. – [www.egypttoday.com].

Business Monthly – from the American Chamber – [www.amcham.org.eg].

Cairo Times – useful paper published every other week – [www.cairotimes.com].

The Croc – useful free guide for the younger set– [www.cairocafe.com.eg].

Community Times – free local paper –
[www.commtimes.com].

Other sources
[Snoopy.tblc.lib.fl.us/utlibrary/Egypt.htm].

[www.chevening.fco.gov.uk].

[www.dtid.gov.uk].

[www.eyp.co.uk]

[Hoovers.com] provides information on specific
companies, both public and private, in great detail.
Search for 'Egypt' at their Website to access all profiles of
larger companies with businesses in Egypt.

[www.MiddleEastWire.com]

[www.brittrade.com/egypt]

[www.british-airways.com/regional/cairo/index-
nsd.shtml]

www.news.bbc.co.uk/hi/arabic/news]

Egyptian Ministry of Tourism home page-
[www.interoz.com/ egypt/index.htm]; [www.touregypt.net]

Construction companies – [www.rccnet.net]

Link to Egypt – [www.eceb-usa.org/elink.html]

Egyptian Economic Bulletin – very useful economic site –
[www.economic.idsc.gov.eg]

Egyptian Internet Business Mall – [www.ibm-e.com]
Investing in Egypt – [www.163.121.10.41/Invest].

Egypt Yellow Pages – [www.egyptyellowpages.com.eg].

Egypt Information Highway – [www.idsc.gov.eg].

Cairo and Alexandria – general information with maps –
[www.pharos.bu.edu/Egypt].

3

getting to Egypt

getting to Egypt

Various considerations in
arranging travel to Egypt.

The tourist heading for Egypt now has a plethora of package tour operators and travel agencies to choose from. The business visitor, however, has particular requirements and will need to make a considerable number of arrangements before departure, if the trip is to repay the investment in time and resources.

Trade Missions

One option for the first-time business visitor to Egypt is to join one of the many regular trade missions to the country. One advantage of joining such a group is that they will organise flights, hotels, transport and visas, another is that in many cases they will have government financial support for the trip. Missions, especially those that accompany a government official, will also have an organised programme of events including meetings with Egyptian officials and senior businessmen, dinners and other social/business events. Ministerial missions will usually have a pre-departure briefing and, some months after the trip, a debriefing in the UK to report back on the success or otherwise of the visit.

Trade missions will usually be accompanied by someone from the organising body – trade association or chamber of commerce. This person will be responsible for ensuring that the group is in the right place at the right time. They will reconfirm flights and transport arrangements. They will often know whom the businessman should contact, and how to get around town. They will be able to advise on etiquette and will deal with local problems as they arise. All very comforting for a first time visitor.

Visas

Visas are required for Egypt. They can be bought in London at the Egyptian Embassy or can be bought upon arrival at the airport. The rate for a visa in London varies according to the duration of stay, whether the visa is for tourism or business and whether multiple entry to Egypt is required. The visa purchased at Cairo airport costs $15, lasts for one visit only of less than a month, does not distinguish between tourists and business visitors and is obtained from the bank kiosks inside the

3

airport. Travel agents, especially those specialising in business travel, will usually arrange to obtain visas prior to departure.

Cairo Airport

If the airport at Cairo seems at first sight a little chaotic, this is possibly a fair impression. After leaving the aircraft, passengers stream through the concourse where they will see an army of agents meeting travellers off the plane. If a visa (postage stamps to be stuck into the passport) is required, now is the time to get it, either with an agent's assistance or directly from the bank kiosk. Queuing and frustration now follows for passport control. Two Egyptian pounds are required for a luggage trolley, available by the carousels. A small scrum follows to get through customs – there is no such thing as 'nothing to declare' – and out into the arrivals hall. March resolutely through avoiding any offers of assistance from would be taxi drivers and 'porters'. A taxi is probably required next and there is an orderly queue of black Mercedes cars of a certain age waiting to take the passenger into Cairo at a fixed charge of 40–50 Egyptian pounds for central Cairo. There are newer white 'limos' also available but their cost is much higher. The local black and white taxis generally overcharge and can be very expensive.

Whichever taxi you take, be prepared for a nerve-racking experience. Late at night when most flights from Europe arrive, the roads are relatively quiet and the drivers keen to deposit their fares as quickly as possible. On the other hand, you should arrive at your hotel relatively quickly.

Travel to Cairo

Most European airlines fly direct to Cairo from their capitals. British Airways flies daily from London, leaving Heathrow in the late afternoon and arriving in Cairo just before midnight local time. Egyptair also has a daily flight leaving slightly earlier. Both flights are adequate in the tourist or economy class, although the refreshments are more substantial on BA, which also serves alcohol. The BA business or first class is very comfortable and offers good service – at a price. Business class tickets are generally one price and it is difficult to get any significant discount on the £1,600 ticket. Tourist class tickets are heavily discounted at flight agencies and prices in the region of £200 are often obtainable. Other airlines have daily or less frequent connections from London to Cairo and can offer tourist class passengers large discounts – some as low as £170 return. All tickets cover airport taxes in London and Cairo. It is worth noting that return tickets bought in Cairo cost significantly more due to the imposition of a sales tax.

Charter flights to Egypt are frequent and fly direct to the tourist resorts of Sharm el Sheikh, Hurghada and Luxor, as well as Cairo. There are also some international flights to Alexandria, including one from London operated by British Airways.

Travel agents who cater for the corporate market will probably expect the business traveller to travel on a business class ticket. Special reductions and offers are few, but they do offer travellers additional services including visas and advice on the country. Cheap tickets are advertised in the travel sections of weekend newspapers but usually carry restrictions on dates and length of stay.

Hotels

Hotels should be booked before departure, especially if a particular hotel or location is essential.

Many hotels will offer to meet the traveller at the airport and transport them to their hotel. Travel agencies such as American Express will also 'Meet and Greet' by arrangement in advance.

Money

Take some cash – US dollars or sterling – with you to Egypt. An entry visa at the airport requires hard currency. It is unlikely that travel agents or exchange bureaux in Europe will have Egyptian pounds available for exchange, so get them from the Egyptian bank kiosks inside the airport.

3

Alternatives to the 'plane

Until recently a car ferry existed between Alexandria and Brindisi in Italy, but this no longer runs. However, there are ferries – both passenger and car – from Nuweiba on the east coast of Sinai to Aqaba in Jordan. It is then possible to drive through Jordan, Syria and Turkey – subject to current travel advice from locals and the FCO. There are ferries from Israel to Europe but driving from Egypt into Israel is not recommended and the route via Aqaba into Jordan and Syria is preferable. Another option is to drive west from Egypt into Libya and on to Tunisia where again ferries to Europe exist. There are also occasional ferries from Port Said to Cyprus, which seem to operate at certain times of the year – it is very difficult to get reliable information about these.

In 1929 it was possible to travel from London to Cairo in a week by train, with a first class sleeper and Pullman supplement for a cost of £32 12s 6d. Today, the nearest you can get to Cairo by train from London is Tartous in Syria, via Istanbul and Aleppo. However, it would take a lot longer, be considerably more expensive and considerably less comfortable. There are prospects of a North African Railway, which would join the European network at Tartous in Syria; already the rail bridge over the Suez Canal, destroyed during the wars with Israel, is under reconstruction. A rail link through Tunisia and Libya and along the north coast of Egypt exists, but needs upgrading. To the east of the Suez Canal, the railway is planned to continue through north Sinai along the route of the old Palestine railway. The complete network would link North Africa with Gaza, Israel, Lebanon and Syria.

Health

Egypt has a reputation as an unhealthy place to visit. In many respects this is well-earned; pollution can be bad, weather can be hot and conditions may not always be as hygienic as one would wish. Doctors and health clinics in Europe and America will advise a number of inoculations. Travel companies, British Airways for example, offer medical services, and the World Health Organisation publishes medical advice to travellers. Long-term protection against typhoid, hepatitis and tetanus is worth considering for regular travellers, and there are occasional outbreaks of polio and meningitis.

Once the business traveller is in Egypt the biggest issue is the cleanliness of food and drink. Careful attention to hygiene, avoidance of some foods (especially uncooked vegetables and salads) and strict abstinence from anything but bottled water should ensure a healthy stay in Egypt.

Travel Insurance

Most travellers and executives are covered either through their own company medical schemes or through the prudent use of credit cards. Travel agents will offer cover for those who wish to be fully insured against health problems or losses during a visit.

Planned meetings before Departure

3

It is advisable for any business visitor to Egypt to arrange some core meetings before arrival. The commercial section of the embassy in Cairo will help direct the newcomer and advise old hands on the current political, and commercial state of the country.

Some executives will have had a sector survey carried out by the embassy before arrival in Cairo and will probably have received a list of names to contact for appointments.

Making the embassy aware that you are in the country is also useful from the standpoint of personal security, especially in periods of political instability.

Once in Cairo, and having contacted the embassy, the **British Egyptian Business Association** or the **American Chamber of Commerce** could be other early calls.

It is not necessary to arrange a full programme of events before arrival. Indeed as we shall see, it could prove costly. Traffic conditions in Cairo are the first obvious restriction on the number of meetings in a day, and it would be unwise to commit oneself to any organisation or individual before the market is thoroughly explored and understood – despite possible glowing letters of introduction.

What to take

Apart from the usual travel documents little else need be taken except for business documents and literature. Many businessmen take laptop computers for their communication purposes – short-term links to local ISP in Cairo are possible. GSM mobile phones now work in many places in Egypt including Cairo and Alexandria. Cameras can be taken in at will, although video cameras or camcorders can cause customs officers to pause for thought. Customs authorities may question the content of videocassettes and some magazines or literature.

An international driving licence is required to drive in Egypt and can be obtained from driving organisations in the UK or US.

Although the pharmaceutical industry in Egypt is advanced, some specialised medicines may be hard to find.

If you want to take a present, consider alcohol (if appropriate), western chocolates and luxury foods. Although these may be available in Egypt, they will generally be expensive, difficult to obtain and not always fresh.

3

4

the ground rules

the ground rules

This section takes the reader by the hand and talks through the nitty-gritty of everyday life, from how to get around to how much to tip the bell-boy.

The majority of business in Egypt revolves around Cairo, and although there are major industrial centres in Alexandria most businesses, ministries and prospective clients have an office in Cairo. There is a trend for companies to move out of the centre to the suburbs of the city and into the satellite cities located around the ring road.

Having arrived in Cairo, the task facing the business traveller is to get about this confusing city in comfort and safety. To make the most of the visit, accommodation, transport, money and customs need to be mastered.

Personal Finances

Credit cards

Credit cards are becoming more and more acceptable, especially in Cairo and Alexandria and in the major hotels throughout Egypt. It is worth checking at remote or cheaper hotels if credit cards are accepted and if so which ones – some are disliked because of the charges levied. There are also some bank cash points in Cairo and Alexandria – but they are not on every street corner and cannot be relied upon to have money or to be working!

Cash and the Egyptian currency

The local currency is the Egyptian pound (LE) which is theoretically allowed to float freely and has remained stable against the US dollar for many years. It does fluctuate slightly against other currencies as a result of changes in the international value of the dollar. One Egyptian pound (LE1) is approximately equivalent to 3.4 US dollars or 5.6 pounds sterling. It is worth noting that in 1980 one Egyptian pound was almost equivalent to one pound sterling, a rapid decrease in value of the Egyptian pound occurring in the mid-eighties.

Payments for most things will be made in local currency. Hotels will probably advertise their room rates in US dollars, but these days will usually take any currency. In fact, the Egyptian pound is exchangeable anywhere, although it is still difficult to obtain Egyptian pounds outside Egypt.

Other places that will demand hard currency are the hotel casinos (only open to foreigners with non-Egyptian passports) and the Duty Free shops.

Money

4

Money

Currency

The Egyptian currency is generally in paper notes – LE1, 5, 10, 20, 50 and 100. Care should be taken with some notes which are remarkably similar – LE10 and LE50 (both maroon) and the LE20 and some LE100 notes (pale green). The pound is divided into piastres, with 100 piastres being equivalent to one pound. There are 50, 25, 10 and even 5 piastre notes, and 20, 10, and 5 piastre coins. The 25 piastre coin has a hole in the middle – much loved by collectors of change as it fits nicely on to a piece of string.

Banks and Exchanges

Currency exchange offices exist in most hotels, certainly the larger ones. It is possible to get hotels to change money through their own cashiers if the formal exchange banks are not available or are closed. The American Express Bank, one of the major hotel banking outlets in Cairo will, subject to its own conditions, cash personal cheques. There are two British banks represented in Cairo: Barclays and the Egyptian British Bank (HSBC); both have UK staff working there. The Americans are represented by the Egyptian American Bank, American Express Bank, Chase Manhattan, Citibank and the Misr America International Bank.

Transport

As everywhere, modern motorised transport is the norm in Egypt although donkeys, mules, horses and camels are widely used in agriculture and in the desert. The sight of herds of camels being driven to market through the streets of Cairo is not uncommon.

Most business travellers to Egypt are likely to travel around by road, either taxi or hired car. Despite the chaos and the age of the vehicles, serious accidents causing personal injury are few within the city.

Taxis

No traveller to Egypt is likely to leave without having experienced at least one journey in an Egyptian taxi. The more luxurious Mercedes taxis are used from the airport, while the regular taxis in Cairo and elsewhere in the country are generally much older and more basic. Taxis in Cairo are

4

easily recognisable – they are black and white. In Alexandria they are yellow and black, and intercity taxis are usually white. Taxis also have distinctive red number plates.

Egypt operates a 'service' taxi system. This means that a taxi will pick up various passengers throughout its journey, so travellers should not be surprised if they find their taxi stopping to pick up additional passengers. A Western passenger is unlikely to share his taxi as the driver will be expecting to receive a much larger fare than from an Egyptian.

Taxi Fares

Taxis have meters which, by law, must work – but even when they do, they are almost never switched on. It is advisable, before getting into a taxi (especially one of the taxis waiting outside hotels), to negotiate a price for the journey. If a fare is not negotiated, the driver will attempt to get as much as he can at the end of the trip. Taxis from hotels are generally dramatically more expensive than one hailed in the street, however, they can be expected to be cleaner and more mechanically reliable. Business travellers expecting to take a large number of taxi rides should negotiate a daily or half-daily rate with a single taxi driver who will usually be happy to come to some such arrangement. It may be possible to develop a relationship with a good driver, for return visits to Egypt. Hotels will monitor the movement of their guests by taxi and doormen can also advise on suitable fares for journeys.

4

Private or Hired Car

Outside the maelstroms of Cairo and Alexandria, driving in Egypt is easy – but very dangerous at night. Roads in Egypt are adequate, although the surface usually leaves a lot to be desired. Vigilance is required but traffic volumes are minimal, especially in Sinai and Upper Egypt.

Car hire is possible from most of the major hotels and airports. An international driving licence is needed and payment may be required in a hard currency. Proof from the hirer that the car is indeed on hire to that driver is sometimes demanded at the infrequent police checks in the country; these are more common in Sinai in the vicinity of Sharm el Sheikh.

Transport

Fuel stations are frequent, especially in urban areas, but it is essential to keep a full tank when heading for remote areas and to carry spare cans if embarking upon desert travel. The hire of 4x4 vehicles for desert trekking is possible, but inadvisable for newcomers without a guide to Egypt.

Buses

Groups of business travellers are often transported from meeting to meeting in modern, air-conditioned tourist buses, many made in Egypt and powered by compressed natural gas. There are also intercity coaches, known as Super Jet Buses, which offer cheap and comfortable travel between Cairo and Alexandria. Intercity buses from Cairo to Luxor, Aswan, Hurghada, Sharm el Sheikh and other major towns exist and are quite satisfactory, although they are slow compared to air services.

Business travellers are unlikely to use the large red and cream public buses in Cairo, or the similar service in Alexandria. The smaller 'micro' buses, whose vehicles and drivers tend to be dangerous, should be avoided, as should the intercity Peugeot 505 estates known with some justification as 'flying coffins'.

Trains

For journeys to Alexandria, the train is the best method of transport. The expresses between the two cities are fast, punctual, comfortable, air-conditioned and offer refreshments brought to the passenger. Fares are minimal and most business travellers will travel first class. Tickets are best bought several days in advance of the journey as these trains get very full and the actual process of purchase can be time-consuming and frustrating – Cairo central railway station is very confusing! Until recently it was only possible to book a ticket and seat in one direction, i.e. a traveller would have to book his return seat from Alexandria to Cairo on his arrival in Alexandria which, with the busy trains, was not always possible.

Trains operate between Cairo and Upper Egypt – Luxor and Aswan. First class sleeper trains cover this journey overnight in about 12 hours – a journey time hardly changed in 80 years. Daytime direct trains are acceptable but take care to avoid the stopping services.

4

Train services elsewhere in the country are strictly for the locals or the railway enthusiast. There are services to Suez and into the Delta. Trains occasionally run along the north coast, waiting for the day when direct links to Sinai, Gaza, Israel, Lebanon, Syria and London are resumed.

Air travel

For the increasing numbers of business travellers wishing to do business outside Cairo, air travel is a better option than the train, except between Cairo and Alexandria. Travel within Egypt is usually by Egyptair, although there are private airlines – one operates between Cairo and El Gouna resort on the Red Sea. Oil companies have their own services. It is also possible to charter planes from Cairo for executive travel.

Possible suggestions are

❑ Alkan Air, tel: (02) 3653702/3490140, fax: 3499253.
❑ Astra Travel, tel: (02) 3446445/3039132, fax: 3036767.

Internal travel via Cairo airport can be confusing. Apart from international Terminals One and Two, there are two other terminals adjacent to Terminal One. It is from these smaller terminals that most internal flights originate.

Flights within Egypt are not cheap and are usually full and their timing cannot be relied upon. Business travellers should allow themselves plenty of time at each end of flights – do not work to a very tight schedule.

Boats
Travel within Egypt by boat is limited to river and lake cruising. The ferry across Lake Nasser from Aswan to Wadi Halfa in Sudan sometimes operates, depending on the current state of relations between Egypt and Sudan.

Communications
In recent years communications in Egypt have improved enormously. Two mobile phone networks arrived in the late nineties, and, with the introduction of a GSM network, mobile phones from other countries may be used.

Transport

4

There are still too many people wanting phone services, both terrestrial and mobile. The private sector companies try to cope with the demand for lines, and the state phone system struggles. While the cost of local calls is negligible, international calls, both to and from Egypt are expensive. The cost of these calls are unlikely to change until the state system is taken over by the private sector.

Mobile Phone Fever

The Egyptians have taken to the mobile phone with enormous enthusiasm. During summer holidays when the people of Cairo descend upon the normally quiet coastal resorts, such is the volume of calls that inevitably the whole system crashes.

In cinemas calls are made – probably in the boring bits – and full conversations carried out. In restaurants the sound of the mobile phone is pervasive. At business seminars and conferences, especially those attended by important people, anybody who thinks they are anybody demands constant calls on their phones. Even in small business meetings be prepared for your contact's inside pocket to emit some strange semi-musical jingle.

However, help is at hand. The Opera House now detaches any mobile phone from its owner before allowing admission – promises of good behaviour fall on deaf ears. Restaurants too are offering a similar service to more discerning or romantic customers.

4

The postal service is at its best slow, and at its worst, erratic and unreliable. As ever, major courier companies operate, with a once- or twice-daily international delivery rate. Services like Aramex, DHL, EMS, IML, Middle East Couriers, SOS Sky International, TNT Skypack, UPS and World Courier are used for world-wide deliveries, and even within Egypt and Cairo itself.

Many ISP companies like InTouch (❏ tel: 02 3311800), Internet Egypt (❏ tel: 02 3563560) and Menanet (❏ tel: 02 4166200) will offer temporary services for avid internet watchers.

People, Practices and Rules

Business in Egypt is conducted in a fairly straightforward manner. There are few pitfalls for the foreign business executive: no sheep's eyes, no sitting cross-legged on the floor, no bowing. Egyptians, unlike most Arabs, do not seem too offended by being shown the soles of one's shoes, although anyone who sits in such a casual fashion in a stranger's presence may expect raised eyebrows.

There is a more relaxed attitude to time than Europeans are accustomed to. Meetings in Egypt tend to start later than expected; the more important the person you are visiting, the later he is likely to be. Invariably the traffic will be blamed for any delay although this is not a recognised excuse from visitors, who should endeavour to be on time. Since the advent of the mobile phone warnings of delays are more often given, and a generally more punctual approach to appointments seems to be developing.

Punctuality

Borrowed Arabic

The Arabic word for tea is *chai* or *shai* – this is similar to the Indian and Chinese words for tea and not too dissimilar to the English word 'char'. It seems that the British in years past took the word back with them to blighty. While they were at it they borrowed a few more words: *gaffer* or foreman, *bint* daughter or girl, and possibly even *eh*, the colloquial Arabic for 'what'.

4

It is worth remembering that in the summer months, business people in Cairo tend to work a shorter week. Affluent Cairenes commonly send their families to the Mediterranean coast for the summer months where many have second homes. Since Saturday often becomes a day off, and since Thursday (the day before the weekend) is often taken as little more than a half-day, the working week is dramatically shortened. The means effectively there are only four working days in the week during the months of June to September.

Work in summer

Before starting a meeting coffee or tea will be offered. Coffee (*ahwa*) is usually of the Turkish type and is more likely to be served in more important offices. There will usually be a glass of (bottled) water provided with the coffee, although in a big meeting there may not be one each. Tea is served without milk, with a lot of sugar and in a small glass. Instant coffee, generally known as 'Nescafé', is now increasingly offered, and soft drinks – Coke, 7-Up or similar – are usually available. The Egyptians make a very refreshing lemon drink out of a unique small local lemon – this is very acceptable if offered. Herbal teas may be offered, but this is rare.

Pleasantries

Meetings will usually start, as in most countries, with a few pleasantries and a handshake. In Europe and America our handshakes tend to be a little perfunctory. In the Middle East and Egypt when shaking hands do not be in a hurry to finish the contact. Introductory topics of conversation can be the traffic problems or English football – both quite acceptable topics – the Egyptians often follow British football with great enthusiasm. During this time the tea boy will take orders. Once the meeting has started it is probable that the tea boy will reappear with the drinks and and interrupt discussions. The telephone too is likely to ring throughout a meeting – this is now getting worse with the use of mobile phones. People tend to arrive and depart throughout proceedings although more serious discussions will be conducted in closed meetings.

It is possible that relatively junior employees will be the ones to welcome the visitors and get the pleasantries out of the way, allowing the decision maker to arrive with the maximum impact when everyone else is settled. *Majlis* (meeting room) type meetings are common in some parts of the Middle East, where the important person will conduct several meetings at the same time, are very uncommon in Egypt.

Dress

There is no special **dress code** for business meetings other than the obvious conventions of being smartly and modestly dressed. Suits for men are usual, although a blazer would be acceptable; an open-necked shirt too casual, certainly for a first meeting. Female executives should dress carefully, with at least half-length sleeves covering arms and reasonably lengthed skirts – trousers would be acceptable. Egyptian Muslim women, even in offices, often wear a head scarf.

Receptions last for about two hours and, while requiring formal dress, are fairly relaxed and useful occasions.

Alcohol is usually served. Formal dinners and luncheons often start later than advised but tend to finish very promptly when the guest of honour departs followed by the rest of the guests. No special formalities are observed, although there will probably be a top table to which dignitaries will be invited.

Religious Etiquette and Ramadan

It is unlikely for a meeting in Egypt to be interrupted by prayers; it is however, possible that appointments will be arranged to suit prayer times. Muslims will pray anywhere, even in the office or in the streets and sensitivity and respect from Western travellers is strongly advised. However, for the month of Ramadan praying and religious observance takes on a more significant role in everyday life.

Five Pillars of Islam

The religious duties of the Muslim are premised upon what are known as the Five Pillars of Islam:

- the *Shahadatayn* or Oral Confession: 'There is no God but God, and Mohammed is His apostle';

- the duty to pray five times a day: at dawn, midday, afternoon, sunset and before retiring for the night;

- the requirement to fast during the holy month of Ramadan;

- the duty to offer *zakat* or alms to the poor, to the value of 2.5 per cent of surplus income;

- the duty for each person to try to perform Haj – the pilgrimage to Makkah – at least once during a lifetime.

The call to prayer echoes out from the minarets mosques at each prayer time. Its mounting call can be heard from every side, the voices of the *muezzin* varying in tone and clarity, each with the same words, beginning: *Allahu Akbar, Allahu Akbar, Ash-shadu an la illah illa Allah; Mohammed Rasoul Allah:* God is Great, God is Great, There is no God but God, and Mohammed is His Prophet.

4

Hijra Calendar

In addition to the Gregorian calendar used throughout the world, the Middle East and the Islamic world in general also observes the Islamic or *Hijra* calendar. Calculated from the Prophet Muhammed's flight to Madinah, it is about 600 years later than the Western system so that year 1999 is equivalent to year 1420 in the Islamic calculation. The calendar is based upon the cycle of the moon, so that each Islamic year is 13 days fewer than the Western year. In Egypt the Islamic calendar is rarely used except for the month of Ramadan.

Ramadan

Muslims observing Ramadan will not eat, drink or smoke during daylight hours. Therefore, they will eat before sunrise and will not break their fast again until after sunset. The evening meal or *iftar* is a happy occasion and is often a meal to share with friends, colleagues and business associates, including foreigners. Guests will arrive just before sunset to a subdued and quiet atmosphere followed shortly afterwards by the announcement that the official fasting period is over and the eating and drinking can begin. These meals only last a short while as most people will want to return home or to their office so in the middle of the night a further, heavier meal is taken, to which guests may also be invited.

4

Ramadan

Ramadan can be a frustrating time for anyone trying to conduct business. Activities for everybody, Muslims, Christians, Egyptians and foreigners alike, suffer enormously during the day. Lack of sleep and excess of food at night leaves everybody very jaded. Offices invariably start late and in order to be ready for *iftar* everybody must be home punctually.

At the end of Ramadan are three days of public holiday. These three days often extend to a full week – a similar phenomenon to the long holidays enjoyed at Christmas in the West. This holiday is known as the *Eid al Fitr* and is followed about two months later by *Eid al Adha* which lasts for slightly longer and is the time in which Muslims may go to Makkah to carry out their holy pilgrimage or *Hajj*.

During Ramadan most Muslims will be sympathetic to the Western business traveller and may offer refreshments during the day. This is one occasion when it would be more understanding for the visitor to decline. Travellers should not smoke, drink or eat in public during daylight hours. Modesty in dress should be especially observed during this holy month.

Tipping

Backsheesh, as it is known, is given for any service and is often expected for no service at all. A fifty piastre or one pound tip is appropriate for insignificant services and to get rid of pestering children – although this sign of weakness may have the opposite effect. More is expected at hotels and for more substantial work performed.

Backsheesh

● At the airport – LE1 per case up to LE5. More might be given if the porter has a long wait or long walk to the car.

● Parking the car – LE1–2. If the area is a downtown street where parking is difficult, this should be raised to at least LE5 to ensure co-operation on return visits.

● Fast food or general deliverers should be tipped at a rate that will ensure good repeat service – if you want your pizza delivered hot next time!

● Toilet attendants will expect up to LE1.

● Taxis from the street will usually charge the traveller a premium rate, so no tip is required. The passenger of a hired car with a driver might give LE5.

● In a five-star hotel allow at least LE5 to have luggage delivered or removed. Waiters are often covered by the service charge levied on most bills, although exceptional or good service should be rewarded. Remember to leave something for the room cleaners at the end of your stay.

Public Holidays

Egypt uses the two calendar systems, Islamic and Western. It has Islamic holidays and also has holidays whose date refers to the Gregorian calendar. This inevitably leads to confusion since one set of holidays move each year with the Islamic calendar and the others do not. Overleaf are the holidays for the next four years.

4

Annual Festival	Approximate dates			
	2000	2001	2002	2003
Holy Fast of Ramadan	27 Nov	16 Nov	5 Nov	25 Oct
Eid al Fitr (end of Ramadan)	7-9 Jan	27 Dec	16 Dec	5 Dec
Eid al Adha (Feast of the Sacrifice)	16-19 Mar	5 Mar	22 Feb	11 Feb
Ras As-Sana (Muslim New Year)	6 Apr	26 Mar	15 Mar	4 Mar
Mawlid An-Nabi (Prophet Muhammad's Birthday)	14 Jun	3 Jun	23 May	12 May
Sham al Nessim (date dependent on Coptic Easter) Year 2000 - 1 May				

The following dates are constant in the Gregorian calendar:

Sinai Liberation Day	25 April
Labour Day	1 May
Revolution Day	23 July
Armed Forces Day	6 October

Weather

Weather in Egypt is very predictable. Hot in summer, mild in winter and with little rain.

Temperatures (celsius)

	June – Sept	Nov – March
Cairo	35-38	10-18
Alexandria	30-35	5-15
Aswan	35-45	18-30

Humidity is generally low, but higher near the sea. Values of 30-60% might be expected.

One phenomenon unique to Egypt are the *Khamseen* winds that come each year in the Spring – any time between February and April. They are unpleasant, bring sand and dust into the cities and make driving dangerous, especially in the desert.

5

getting down to business

getting down to business

This chapter provides elementary guidance on the basic etiquette of business, and also contains details of useful local organisations who can assist with the more complicated requirements of business transactions.

Agents and Local Partners

Companies wishing to export to Egypt must, by law, have an agent if they are selling to the public sector and must be registered with the Ministry of Trade and Supply. To trade with the private sector such an arrangement is not absolutely necessary and a local associate can look after the company's affairs, both legal and commercial. Some companies coming to Egypt will not need an agent; although consultants, investors and contractors can in theory operate on their own, it is likely that they will need a local partner. For example, contractors must award more than 50 per cent of a contract to local companies; only local consultants can give final approval for construction.

Companies should of course choose their local partner with care. The difficulties of parting company with an agent who turns out to be unsuitable are enormous, with the benefit of the doubt always given to the local party.

There are also Egyptian entrepreneurs who will offer themselves as go-betweens to sort out problems and to make the necessary introductions. This role is becoming less necessary with greater transparency in awarding tenders.

Sometimes circumstances outside anyone's control dictate that an association should be formed with a certain Egyptian company. Often when large international contracts are to be awarded a local entrepreneur may contact a construction company or specialised supplier directly. For example, when the pumping station for the Toshka project was first suggested, there was a rush by individuals in Egypt to arrange joint ventures with international companies. Contractors, both local and international and the few international pump manufacturers in the world who could supply the equipment, were all contacted in order to form a winning group.

Very often, as in this example, there are only few specialised companies who could qualify. In the case of the pumps for Toshka only one international manufacturer was fully compliant. Sometimes the competition is limited by a very tight specification being written by the client's consultant. Indeed it is sometimes possible to ensure that the client and his consultant are

5

Tendering on major contracts

75

so impressed by certain equipment that they will either specify it directly or write a specification so that only this one manufacturer can comply. This writing of specifications around a certain piece of equipment by a client is not uncommon and is particularly relevant where a client wants a certain item but the rules of tendering by a government, a bank or another loan agency prevent the use of preferential suppliers. American and European aid agencies are particularly strict with their rules for loans and grants.

It might be that the executive has come to Cairo with a specific goal in mind. He or she may have come to influence the donors of finance or the government body who will benefit from this money. The executive may therefore need to see his existing agent and also make presentations to the local consultant or government office. When making presentations it is worth remembering that Egyptian officials are often very technologically sophisticated. CD-ROM driven presentations can easily be made and should be used for the greatest impact, although it is advisable to check that viewing and projection equipment is available.

However, in many cases the business visitor will be making a first trip with a list of prospective agents already drawn up and one or all of them previously contacted. It is worth commenting that sometimes local agents endeavour to include all possible suppliers of a product or service in their portfolios so that they can monopolise the market. Advice about agents and the local market will obviously be a priority for a newcomer and sources of information are given below. Sources of statistical information are numerous but the executive should be cautious about the reliability and validity of statistics, especially official government figures which are often several months in arrears; unofficial sources can often give a more accurate and up-to-date assessment.

5

Choosing a local partner

Government Regulation and Import Controls

The Egyptian government regularly restructures regulations to safeguard Egyptian business and of the country in general. Following the Far Eastern crash of

1998, for example, it became more difficult to import goods into the country as there was a fear that raw materials and goods would be dumped on the Egyptian market. While outright restrictions were not imposed, stricter customs controls were enforced, foreign currency became more difficult to obtain, bank loans for speculative building were discouraged and letters of credit required funds in the bank to guarantee payment.

There are good shipping agents in Egypt accustomed to working with the regulations. Most have offices in Cairo and Alexandria and some companies have offices at the international land frontiers with Libya and Israel. Large Egyptian agents also have offices or associates overseas and some will be able to consolidate shipments from overseas to Egypt, offering a door-to-door service.

The newcomer to the market should use a well known agent in Egypt to handle all shipments both in and out of the country. Advice on specific agents can be obtained from embassies, trade organisations and local businessmen. The temptation to embark upon an association with one of the smaller companies, which might offer better rates, should be resisted. In the long run the straightforward and regular approach to importation is probably the cheapest.

British Embassy

The British Embassy commercial section, in conjunction with British Trade International in London, offers a co-ordinated service, although some of the more time-consuming services and written advice has to be paid for. The section in the Cairo embassy usually has at least two expatriate members of staff, drawn from the Foreign and Commonwealth Office or the Department of Trade and Industry and posted to Egypt for about three years. They are experienced in commercial work, have a good knowledge of the local market and, most importantly, know sources of information. These sources range from lawyers or accountants to agents and suppliers. They can also identify relevant government offices and agencies and even provide names of local dentists and doctors in case of emergency. The Egyptian staff in the commercial section bring an important local dimension to the advice available and the market reports.

Business gatherings

The commercial section also holds an 'at home' gathering at the beginning of each month for the resident business community. Frequently, visiting businessmen attend these informal discussions which are held at the residence of the head of the commercial section.

British Embassy: ❏ Tel: (02) 3540852; fax: (02) 3540859

All nationals of the European Union countries have another source of commercial help, the Commission of the European Union in Zamalek. While it is not an embassy the Commission is a major source of aid and funds from members of the European Union and the local office can offer advice.

European Union Delegue: ❏ Tel: 3400388; fax: 3400385 E-mail: [dece@idsc.gov.eg].

American Chamber of Commerce

AmCham

The American Chamber of Commerce, or AmCham as it is known, is a very powerful organisation in Egypt. AmCham also has offices in Cairo, Washington DC and in Alexandria. The Chamber has committees which represent most business activities in Egypt, including construction, investment, health, shipping, tourism and legal affairs. These groups meet regularly to discuss current concerns and are able to lobby the government on behalf of their members. Politically, AmCham is represented by the Presidents' Council which reports directly to the Presidents of the two countries and numbers the Vice President of the United States in its membership.

AmCham can offer a lot of information about business in Egypt. A glossy magazine, *Business Monthly*, is produced by the Chamber and circulated free of charge to anyone in Egypt who is on their mailing list – members or not. They have a large amount of information on their database of companies and opportunities, and disseminate this through the Internet to their members. Most major companies working in Egypt whether local, American or otherwise are members of this chamber.

AmCham also holds seminars on topics of political, technical or general interest. Visiting business executives are welcome.

5

AmCham: ❏ Tel: (02) 3381050; fax:(02) 3381060
Website: [www.amcham.org.eg]
E-mail: [acce@ritsec1.com.eg]

British Egyptian Business Association

This association is generally known by its acronym BEBA. It was set up to assist the growing number of British businesses in Egypt on the same lines as the AmCham but without the financial resources. BEBA, like its wealthy cousin, has sector committees and produces a regular newsletter. Full time staff in the BEBA offices in Agouza can offer advice, information and introductions.

The Egyptian British Business Council (EBBC) was formed as a result of a visit by the British Prime Minister to Egypt and BEBA. The EBBC has a similar role to that of the AmCham's Presidents' Council and includes the Prime Ministers of Egypt and the UK.

BEBA holds regular business lunches where senior Egyptian officials will speak. They are well attended by representatives from the Egyptian and British business communities.

❏ Tel: (02) 3491401; fax: (02) 3491421; on their website: [www.beba.com]; e-mail: [egyptuk@beba.com]

The Egyptian Exporters Association (ExpoLink)

This organisation is particularly useful for those travellers who might have come to Egypt to buy local products for an overseas market: ExpoLink is a privately funded organisation founded to increase exports and takes part in trade fairs and promotions (24 in 1999) around the world. They are located in new offices in Mohandaseen, where they have the latest IT systems to assist them in their 'match-making' role. They have a wealth of knowledge about local companies.

ExpoLink focuses its services on five sectors – ready-made clothes, footwear and leather products, fresh and processed food, furniture, and information technology. It offers a one-stop shop service for Egyptian international trade.

BEBA

EBBC

5

In addition to direct export promotion activities they are able to assist with training and staff development. Funds from the European Union and the United States of America are available to support such programmes and the Department of Trade and Industry (DTI) in the UK support through its Hands On Training Scheme (HOTS).

BEBA: ❑ Tel: (02) 3046886; fax: (02) 3046889
E-mail: [info@expolink]

Other Business Groups in Egypt

The Greeks, Italians, French, Japanese and Germans also have chambers of commerce. Most other countries with any significant trade with Egypt will have an office in Cairo. The Federation of Egyptian Industries has an office on the Nile and the powerful lobby group, the Egyptian Business Association (EBA) has large premises in Giza. Alexandria and other major towns have commercial chambers and the new cities of 6th October and 10th Ramadan have Unions to encourage investors.

EBA

There are many Rotary clubs in Egypt of which two are English-speaking. These groups meet regularly and welcome visits from fellow Rotarians from around the world.

British Council

The British Council is located in Agouza on the west bank of the Nile and was established more than 50 years ago. In recent years a branch of the Council was opened in Heliopolis. The council has a large lending and reference library which also contains videos and cassettes. Information is available about the UK on its Internet services together with a large selection of directories on computers or as hard copy. Newspapers and magazines are also available.

The council runs courses for Egyptians to learn English and for foreigners to learn Arabic. Courses are offered in computer skills. Some major companies use the services of the council to run training programmes in English and other business skills. Training is also offered on a contract basis for agricultural development. They can assist in arranging places at British universities and schools.

5

British Council: ❏ Tel: (02) 3031514; fax: (02) 3443076
E-mail: [british.council@eg.britcoun.org]

United Nations and Other International Agencies

As in many Middle Eastern countries there is a large UN presence: UNICEF, UNDP, UNWRA. Additionally, the IMF, IFC, FAO,WHO and ILO are all represented in Cairo.

As with the European Union it is necessary to register products, interests and skills with most UN agencies. They can then call for a particular product from companies or consultants who have previously qualified.

Information centres

Middle East Library for Economic Services

Government laws, especially those relating to foreign companies and their operation, can be obtained from MELES. This privately run organisation is sponsored by the government and encouraged to make current legislation available to everyone.

MELES 6 Abd al-Aziz Soliman St., Agouza, Cairo.
❏ Tel: (02) 3351141/(02) 3606804; fax:(02) 3606804
Website: [www.meles.com]

5

Central Agency for Public Mobilisation and Statistics

CAPMAS is one of several government agencies which record and compile official government statistics. Some of the more useful information they produce is translated into English.

The Egyptian Centre for Economic Studies

ECES is an independent non-research institute which was founded in 1992 by members of the private sector business community. Its objective is to promote economic development in Egypt by assisting policy makers and the business community in identifying and implementing reform. It aims to understand the economic problems facing Egypt and by carrying out research and distributing this information, hopes to develop a better understanding of and hence solutions to these problems. ECES circulates its publications and holds lectures, conferences and discussion groups in its aim to generate discussion about Egypt's economy.

ECES: ❏ Tel: (02) 5781202; fax: (02) 5781205
Website: [www.eces@eces.org.eg]

Governor's offices

The capital of Egypt is divided into two governorates: Cairo, covering the east bank of the Nile and Giza on the west bank. These powerful offices are responsible for all municipal services, planning and civil defence. All major towns in Egypt have governors appointed directly by the President. Each one has a sizeable annual budget and is a potentially valuable client for manufacturers and suppliers of municipal services.

5

6

major industries

major industries

6

An overview of each of the major
industries of the nation and
where they stand today.

Major Industries

At the beginning of 2000, the economy of Egypt is buoyant; privatisation and exports are the main topics of discussion within the business community. The socialist ideals of the fifties linger in some quarters, especially the civil service and the government where the need to keep people in full employment is accepted and wholesale privatisation has not yet been fully implemented. Various schemes, like the Social Fund for Development, have been set up to limit the social and financial hardships that might be brought about as a result of the elimination of overstaffing and the pursuit of increased efficiency.

Economic and social indicators

	1978	1998
Population (m)	38	62
Labour force (m)	9.5	22
Annual average population growth rate (%)	–	2+
Life expectancy (years)	–	67
Electricity consumption per head (kwh)	350	1,500
Private cars registered	312,000	1,100,000
Main telephone lines per 100 persons	1.3	5.2
Literacy (%)	42	61
Stock market capitalisation ($m)	-	27,500
Unemployment (%)	–	8
Inflation (%)	20	4
Central bank foreign exchange reserves ($bn)	-	16
Current account balance-($m)	–	2,700
GDP growth (%)	–	5+

6

European and American companies are increasing investment in Egypt and developing their businesses by

Investors

taking advantage of Egypt's liberal investment regime. Such companies frequently export their products to a third country. Government incentives, especially tax holidays for investors, together with the large flexible labour force and low inflation make investment in Egypt an attractive proposition. If the prospective investor or industrialist can overcome the hurdles presented by Egypt's legendary bureaucracy, the benefits can be considerable.

In recent years, international buyers have been visiting the country in increasing numbers to purchase products and establish permanent lines of supply despite American import quotas and restrictive EU regulations. Egyptian industry is exporting to the west and some factories are supplying well-known international high street chains with food, food products and ready-to-wear garments. One of the most familiar exports of these items to UK shoppers for a number of years has been the first new potatoes of the season.

Despite the export drive in 1999, Egyptian imports far exceeded exports. Egypt relies upon three major sources of foreign exchange: tourism, canal dues and remittances from Egyptian nationals working outside the country – mainly in Saudi Arabia and the Gulf states.

6

The Migrant Workforce

The migrations of Egyptian expatriate workers, like the movements of swallows in England, herald the seasons of the years. These exiles return at the beginning of June and depart in September. Another indicator of summer is the influx of wealthy tourists from the same region who come to the more hospitable climes of Cairo for its many forms of entertainment. The first thing anybody will notice if they go to Cairo airport during these periods are the hordes of Egyptians who have come to greet family and friends. It is not uncommon for the whole extended family, maybe ten people, to be in the arrival hall waiting for one person. Consider then that at this time the airlines put on many extra flights, possibly five or six instead of one, and it is possible to envisage the size of the crowds that quickly form.

Income from the Suez Canal is generally reliable although it is influenced by fluctuations in world trade, so that when the economy of the Far East declined in 1998, the amount of shipping passing through the canal decreased and revenues dipped.

Tourism is by far the most important source of foreign exchange, and although wealthier visitors with plenty of cash to spend are being targeted, the package tourist is not being forgotten, so that by 1999, more than one hundred new hotels were under construction in Egypt. Events which deter potential tourists, particularly acts of terrorism, can have an immediate and devastating effect on the number of visitors and hence the economy.

Tourism

Quality of tourist

The recent incidents of terrorism in Upper Egypt have naturally had their impact on tourism. Tour prices have been slashed, and the incredible bargains have attracted a new breed of tourist, drawn less by the nation's cultural heritage than by the sun and sand. More importantly, they move thriftily throughout their visit. This is an issue of which the authorities have become increasingly aware, and a move is afoot to try and entice back the big spenders of previous times.

6

Egypt's archaeological tourist attractions are known throughout the world. Perhaps not quite so well known are its thousands of kilometres of beaches and coral reef, which stretch from Libya in the west to Israel in the east and Sudan in the south. In 1986 tourism generated a modest $200m, ten years later this had risen to $3b. By the end of 1999, despite the terrorist campaign centred on Luxor in 1997, tourist numbers had reached nearly four million, although the revenue generated had not recovered to the levels reached before the Luxor incident. This can be explained by the increasing importance of cheap package tours arriving from Europe and Russia.

Tourism

The quality of interior design, landscaping and facilities in Egyptian hotels is outstanding. Competition for contracts between European and American designers and contractors is intense with hotels and beach resorts installing ever more imaginative and luxurious facilities. The hotels themselves are also keen to outdo their rivals with imported materials, marbles, textiles and furniture decorating their establishments. Several new villages or hotel complexes are being developed in various areas around Egypt, each with its own facilities: some have golf courses and one even has its own small airport and brewery.

Diving is the most popular sport around the Red Sea coasts. The southern areas towards Sudan have the most wrecks and coral reefs in the region. Surface water sports are also developing, with wind-surfing, paragliding and many other activities on offer, while back on dry land golf courses are being built in many locations around the country. Even hot-air ballooning, made famous when Egypt became the landing place for the first around the world flight, is gathering supporters. International sports companies are moving in to supply this demanding market.

6

Energy

Egypt is an exporter of oil and oil-related products, which together accounted for about 7 per cent of GDP in 1998. However, in 1999, a small deficit occurred for the first time for several years. The prospects for the country's petrochemical industry remain good with Egypt's oil reserves in 1999 increasing to 8 billion barrels. The largest current project is the $1.3b Midor refinery – a joint venture with Israeli, Italian and French participation which is scheduled to be in production in the year 2000; a polyethylene plant is due for completion shortly after. BP Amoco is probably the largest foreign investor in any sector in Egypt, with Shell, Repsol, Apache, GNR and Elf the other major oil field investors.

Natural gas

The discovery and exploitation of Egypt's **natural gas** resources only seriously started in the late 1980s when incentives were offered to commercial companies to carry out exploration. A major industry has rapidly developed, with British Gas and BP Amoco at the forefront, and other international companies such as Shell, Agip, Mobil and

ENI, taking stakes in new concessions. Even companies from Argentina and China have shown interest in the opportunities. In 1999 Egypt's reserves were estimated at about 37 trillion cubic feet of gas, with potential for a similar amount yet to be discovered. The export of gas to Israel, Jordan, Turkey, Lebanon and Syria, together with a $1b liquefied natural gas plant to supply these markets, is under consideration. The Egyptian Ministry of Electricity, Energy and Power is looking beyond fossil fuels for its power needs in the next millennium and is developing plans for solar and wind power. A BOOT 300 megawat wind farm is planned for the east coast of the country, where high wind velocities are experienced all year around.

Petroleum & Natural Gas				
	1988	1994	1996	1997
Output				
Crude Oil	40	44	43	41
Natural Gas	11	9	10	11
LPG	2	1	1	1
Condensates	1	1	1	2
Processing				
Refinery Output	29	26	28	29
Petroleum Products	28	25	27	28
Consumption				
Petroleum Products	24	18	20	22
Natural Gas	11	9	10	10
Trade in oil and refined products ($m)				
Imports	1,100	800	1,400	1,600
Exports	1,200	2,100	2,700	2,450

Coal is once again being mined in Sinai and small amounts are being exported through El Arish port to Turkey.

6

6

British Gas

My first involvement with the British gas industry goes back twelve years to when I first came to Cairo to work on the Waste Water Project. I lived in the outskirts of Cairo, in Heliopolis, in a flat with natural gas and a gas meter installed under the watchful eye of Brian – I know this because he had signed his name on the meter. It was a surprise that Egypt piped natural gas – having spent years in the region with the ubiquitous blue bottled gas.

Brian, who of course was British, is probably no longer in Egypt but his colleagues and associates from the industry are. British Gas, who have been established here since the 1970s, are currently involved with many projects in the country. They are carrying out exploration in the Mediterranean and Red Seas and in the Western Desert covering an area three times that which British Gas PLC holds in the UK. The industry is currently supplying gas from eighteen fields located in various parts of the country to Cairo, Alexandria and the Delta.

Gas is more environmentally friendly than oil and is more efficient in producing the energy upon which the country depends. Already more than 60 per cent of the electrical power in Egypt is provided from gas-fired power stations. The buses and cars of Cairo are being converted to run on compressed natural gas (CNG) in order to reduce pollution in the city.

Agriculture

In the 1960s agriculture accounted for 30 per cent of GDP and about 70 per cent of Egypt's total exports. Thirty years later the contribution to GDP had decreased to 15 per cent and the exports to a mere 10 per cent, although agriculture still accounts for about 30 per cent of national employment. In the fifteen years between 1980 and 1995 agricultural exports rose from $120m to $500m, whilst imports rose from $400m to a staggering $3,000m in the same period. Most revenue comes from the export of potatoes, citrus fruits and cotton to markets where there is an increasing demand for quality.

Egypt's **food trade deficit** is projected to continue for the foreseeable future. However, a number of major projects are under way to develop areas of the desert into industrial and agricultural production sites.

The development of **North Sinai** is really more of a redevelopment project. This area on the coast of the Mediterranean was once a productive agricultural region, but neglect and the Arab-Israeli conflicts meant that the area was all but lost to the desert. There is now a project to divert fresh water from the Nile to irrigate this land. Although there had been for many years an irrigation canal from Cairo to Ismailia, there was hitherto no way to carry this water across the Suez Canal. A large siphon has now been constructed under the canal allowing water to pass from the west bank to the east and on to re-established canals in Sinai. To facilitate exports, the small port at El Arish on the north west of Sinai is being developed.

The **East Oweinat** project is situated in the far south west of Egypt and bordering Sudan and Libya in the area made famous by the Gebel Oweinat cave paintings in the film *The English Patient.* Two hundred thousand acres of land will be transformed by pumping water from the Nubian aquifer. The soil and air is unpolluted in this area and it is intended to produce quality organic crops on this land for the lucrative western markets. In fact some produce is already being grown and exported to Europe. Overseas involvement in this project includes Australians and Malaysians, as well as European and Middle Eastern investors. Opportunities exist for companies to become involved in the development of roads, power stations (wind farms are particularly favoured in this very hot and windy region) and an airport to export the speciality produce. Post-harvest technology and irrigation systems will also be required in order to maximise quality and output.

It is expected that once this project is complete an additional labour force of 20,000 people will be required in the packaging, harvesting and general agricultural industries. Such a labour force might sustain a resident population of about 100,000.

The **Toshka** or **New Valley** project will supply water from the Nile at Lake Nasser through 300 kilometres of

6

Transforming the desert

canals north west to 600,000 acres of land around the existing oasis of Kharga. The project, initiated in 1997, by President Hosni Mubarak, aims to increase the area of agricultural land in Egypt by 25 per cent over the next twenty years.

It is estimated that the total investment in the Toshka project will be about $90bn (about 5 times the level of Egypt's current GDP). Of this sum about three-quarters will be spent on infrastructure, construction and industrial development, while the remaining funds will go towards agriculture and tourism projects. The Egyptian government is paying about a quarter of the investment – to be spent on the main pumping station at Lake Nasser, roads, power supply and the main canal. In addition the government will be offering subsidies to industries that set up in the area, including a 20 year tax exemption, cheap land and import benefits. It is expected that the building material industry will take advantage of the raw materials in the region to manufacture cement, glass, bricks and ceramics.

6

Private investors including some international groups have made offers for much of the proposed agricultural land. Like East Oweinat, the clean land, the weather and the proximity to water make it a suitable location for organic farming. Farmers will be offered incentives to move from the Delta to this new area.

Opportunities exist for road, rail, airport and power station BOOT projects to supplement the government's contribution and to satisfy the anticipated demand for services from the increased population in the area.

The $500m construction project to build one of the world's largest pumping stations started in 1998. The pumps will lift water 50 metres from Lake Nasser into canals some 300 kilometres in length. Construction of the canals started in 1997 and they are expected to cost another $1b. Branch canals and booster pumping station contracts have yet to be let.

Power for Toshka (200-400 MW) is expected to be provided by a new power station to be built as a BOOT project with oil and gas being supplied from nearby fields. Wind and solar energy sources are also being considered.

Food Industries

The changing tastes of a nation

When I first came to Egypt in 1985 food, a very significant aspect of daily life, was, to say the least, boring. It was back to basics and seasonal changes. Food shopping was dominated by small corner shops, euphemistically called supermarkets, where household items and general food stuffs were available.

There was of course meat; large sections of animals hanging from hooks; fish for sale in the markets around Cairo or from roadside stalls; chickens - usually with their feathers on - which fixed you with a beady eye and sorrowful look when you chose them to grace your dinner table.

Vegetables and fruit were another story however. Strawberries and citrus fruit at Christmas were delicious. Peaches and grapes in the early summer. New potatoes, fresh peas and broad beans all arrived as a seasonal treat. The high summer months were a lean time with little available. Packing, processing and preserving did not exist; tomatoes for example would arrive at the shops having travelled on hot, bumpy and dusty roads heaped in large boxes.

Things have changed. Meat is still available from butchers, but cold stores are much in evidence, and prepacked cuts are available in supermarkets. The main fish market in the centre of Cairo has closed, to be replaced by a modern facility on the outskirts of town.

Vegetables and fruit are now better packed. Kiwi fruit arrives in boxes with individual compartments. Asparagus comes with a ribbon around the bunch. Artichokes are individually wrapped. Mushrooms come in trays covered with clingfilm, grapes in conical paper bags, strawberries in punnets.

Apart from the packaging, a lot of these and other products are new to Egypt. In fact, the country is developing so fast that large supermarkets are now commonplace and, as in Europe, the latest innovation is organic food shops.

6

In the 1940s Egypt was the leading food processing country in the Middle East, but during the 1950s and 1960s, government control restricted the growth of this industry. In recent years the private sector has regained its independence, although the government retains powers of intervention over the price of basic foodstuffs. Investment in the industry is rising and will soon reach an annual figure of $300m.

Rice

Egypt's staple foods are bread and rice. Although Egypt has increased yields of rice significantly in recent years, from 6 tonnes to 8 tonnes per hectare, the country is trying to redirect its limited water resources by growing water efficient crops in new areas. In consequence, future expansion in rice production is not expected to be great.

Sugar

Historically, one of Egypt's major food exports has been high quality sugar from the cane fields and refineries of Upper Egypt. With the need to conserve water, especially for the Toshka project, sugar cane is being replaced by beet sugar. The private sector now controls more than 40 per cent of the 2 million tonne annual production. In 1997 it was estimated that Egyptians consumed 30 kilograms of sugar per person each year.

Flour

More than half Egyptian flour is milled by traditional stone grinding, but there are current plans to radically expand the number of modern mills. In the late 1990s plans to develop modern mills were introduced. Annual consumption of wheat per annum is in excess of 120 kilograms per person, and an increasing demand for higher quality flour for use in bread and processed food will ensure that this sector of the food industry is buoyant for years to come.

Production of convenience foods is rising as the wealth and population of the country increases: the soft drinks industry has grown enormously; the sweet and confectionery industries are expanding; and frozen and preserved produce is now common in local supermarkets – a dramatic development of the last ten years.

Alcohol

Egypt has been producing alcoholic beverages probably since Pharaonic times – longer than anyone else in the world. In the 1950s and 1960s, when the state took over control of the industry, standards

6

declined. In the late 1990s the private sector, with foreign investors and technology, is rejuvenating the production of wine and beer.

Textiles

In the mid 1990s, the value of Egyptian ready-made garments and furnishing fabrics amounted to $1.5b. The textile industry is dominated by two developing trends: increasing private sector involvement, and the growth in production of ready-made garments. The export of garments has increased whilst imports have declined, contributing significantly to the national GDP.

Egyptian Cotton

If you think of cotton, you think of Egypt and in particular long staple cotton, the best and the most durable; the cotton industry in Lancashire, England, was built upon it. After a brief spell when synthetic materials dominated the marketplace, cotton is back.

For some years now cotton clothing shops in Egypt have been selling good quality home-produced goods. So it is no longer merely raw cotton that is exported – finished products are being sold in the west, including the UK. Recently, clothes made from organically-produced cotton have been sold to a British clothing chain store.

The textile industry is not limited to clothes. Luxury fabrics are made for the soft furnishings industry. Western designers are turning to this market hoping to print and weave fabrics in Egypt under licence.

6

Manufacturing

A growing number of multinational companies from America, Europe and the Far East, especially the car and automotive industries, are locating in Egypt. Manufacturing is just less than 20 per cent of total output of which some two thirds is in the private sector. A third of all private investment in Egypt is in manufacturing industries and the government is aiming to withdraw from this sector altogether.

The automotive industry, which includes cars, buses, and lorries has attracted the most foreign investment. Mercedes, General Motors, Peugeot, Suzuki and Hyundai have all been attracted to Egypt. Suppliers to the industry, including Lucas Varity, produce parts in the Cairo Free Zone for export to Europe and America.

Pharmaceutical companies are investing in the country with such names as GlaxoWellcome, Squibb, Bristol Myers and Hoechst. The electronics industry is represented by Far Eastern and European companies. Ceramics are taking off.

Iron ore extraction is taking place in Upper Egypt. Aluminium plants have also been established in this area. Phosphates are mined in southern Egypt and Sinai.

Two new industrial zones are being developed at **East Port Said** and in the **Gulf of Suez**. Each includes a 25 square kilometre port area together with a 90 square kilometre area for industrial development. Whilst Port Said will concentrate on heavy and maritime industries including ship repair, Suez will look more towards industries related to petrochemicals. The Port Said project should benefit from its location at the northern end of the Suez Canal and on the Mediterranean Sea to become a regional hub-port. A fish farming industry and a general commercial area together with limited tourist facilities is also envisaged. Similar plans are being developed for the Suez area, which will also benefit from a new tunnel under the canal linking Suez with the Sinai peninsular.

Education

From the time of President Nasser, Egypt has had strong socialist leanings. In line with this leaning, schools and universities were taken into public ownership. With a few notable exceptions, e.g. the American University, most of the educational establishments were state run. In later years private schools were set up by various religious or ethnic groups – the British, Americans, the French etc. and run as charitable organisations, although still under the supervision of the Ministry of Social Affairs. This continues today but there are now many more, and private schools are common and expensive. In 1998 European countries started to introduce their own universities into the country, led by the British Council.

Environmental and construction Industries

In line with global trends, Egypt has recently become concerned with environmental issues. The establishment of the Ministry of the Environment in 1998 will hopefully ensure the implementation of legislation such as Law Number 4 of 1994, which covered environmental and population issues. Projects to clean polluted waterways are being developed, testing of vehicle emissions has been established, safety in the workplace is under discussion, and National Parks have been established together with special restrictions on building and development on the coast. Wardens have been appointed to monitor protected areas and more parks are planned.

The Zebeleen

It might come as a surprise to learn that Egypt and its people have been involved for many years in environmental projects. In Cairo, rubbish is collected daily by the zebeleen (from the Arabic for rubbish), a Christian sect who jealously guard the right to refuse collection throughout the city. They earn a few pounds a month for this dubious privilege. The zebeleen have been recycling the contents of Cairo's rubbish bins for many years and with their donkey carts and distinctive odour are a familiar sight. Attempts by well-meaning European agencies to improve at least the method of transport have failed – the fuel for motorised trucks cannot be collected from people's rubbish, unlike feed for donkeys.

6

Major waste water and water supply projects have been ongoing since the early 1980s. The Greater Cairo Waste-Water project, involving European and American companies and finance, is not expected to be complete until the second decade of this century.

7

setting up a permanent operation

setting up a permanent operation

The aim of this section is to provide a sweeping overview for the visitor who is considering the possibility of a local office. Here are some of the pitfalls and benefits, an insight into the legal situation, and some of the major issues to be considered, such as recruiting, finding premises, etc.

Opening an Office

Legal Aspects

Egypt suffers from the justified perception that it is awash with bureaucracy. However, when a foreign company wishes to become established in the country the rules are generally straightforward, although it is inadvisable for any foreign company to embark upon the process without professional advice and guidance. There are several lawyers in the country with international reputations and expertise; well-known international accountants and auditors also maintain offices in Egypt. A foreign company may establish a representative office, a branch office or a locally incorporated company.

A **representative office** is the easiest route to pursue, however, such an office is not permitted to carry out any commercial activities or agency operations. The office may carry out feasibility studies or market surveys, but no taxable activities except the payment of salaries. A representative office for a pharmaceutical company may also include a scientific section in which all employees must be Egyptian.

A **branch office** may be opened if the company has a contract with either the private or the public sector to carry out work in Egypt. A branch office can engage in commercial work including financial, industrial and contracting activities although limited to the projects described in the branch registration. The branch registration should be regularly reviewed and updated. Restrictions on the numbers of employees, foreign and local are enforced. Annual audited accounts are required by the authorities and tax inspectors are liable to descend upon the office at any time.

Government approval is required to open a branch office. Approval must be obtained from the Minister of Internal Trade and also the minister responsible for the particular activity the foreign company is involved with. The investment authority (GAFI) must also give its approval and the branch office must be registered in the Commercial Registry. Registration with relevant local unions and associations will also be required. The branch must comply with all Egyptian laws governing taxation, labour, foreign exchange and social insurance.

7

Branch offices

The tax man

In 1986 I was working in an office in Cairo when the tax man called. The visit had been preceded by a hand-written note demanding several million pounds in back taxes for the last ten years. In panic I sought local advice. 'Write back and say it's too much.' This I duly did. Some months later another demand reached my office. While it was still a lot of money it had been reduced. Panic again drove me to my advisor. 'Send it back and say it's too much.' After some further correspondence, the tax authorities decided to visit. The tax man took up residence in our office for three months, poring over ledgers and dusty old books and receipts. Several times a day he raised queries about expenses and projects over the previous ten years – of which I had little knowledge. Finally, the day arrived when the inspector came no more.

Some months later I became concerned about the outcome of the inspector's researches and decided to pay a visit to his office. Little was known. My friend had left the tax office along with all his research into our affairs and was now residing in Saudi Arabia. The whole exercise would have to be repeated.

Foreigners must obtain work and residence permits and may not exceed 10 per cent of the total numbers employed in any office, excluding the branch manager. They, like their Egyptian colleagues, will be expected to pay taxes and social insurance.

As an alternative to a branch or representative office, a foreign company can establish a locally incorporated company. The two most common forms are a joint stock company and a limited liability company. The laws governing these arrangements are the Investment Law, Law number 8 (the Investment and Guarantees Law) and Law number 159 which was amended in 1998 to become Law number 3 (the Companies Law).

Law Number 8: the Investment Law

As its name implies, this law was established to encourage investment in Egypt. By the end of 1998 a total of 1,254 companies, with a capital of LE 45bn had invested over

LE80bn. More than 200 of these companies were from the US and a little fewer than 200 from Britain – although UK companies had invested slightly more. The majority of these companies are involved in manufacturing, with tourism and service companies close behind. Agriculture, construction and finance were other significant sectors. Surprisingly perhaps, approximately one third of the investment went to Alexandria.

The government issues a list of project categories that prospective investment companies must be involved with in Egypt. These include agriculture, tourism, manufacture and mining, oil exploration, aviation and transport services and any projects funded by the Social Fund for Development. Law 8 guarantees against expropriation or nationalisation by the government, and prevents any authority from interfering with the administration of the company. Tax holidays are also granted depending upon the location of the company's activities. These can be for periods of up to twenty years for companies locating in the Toshka and East Oweinat regions.

Law Number 3: the Companies Law

Law number 3, issued in 1998, made it easier for a foreign company to become established in Egypt. Limited documentation has to be submitted by the founders of the company to the Companies Department. The board of the company must consist of directors and must issue a specified number of shares either for public subscription or to private investors. A limited liability company can be established under this law.

Other laws affecting companies operating in Egypt

Law 203 started the privatisation of the state industries. Labour laws have been stream-lined in order to encourage foreign investors, and modernised to provide for healthcare and pensions for all employees. Laws governing land ownership by foreigners do not allow for speculative investment in agricultural land – although special exceptions have been made to this law in the Toshka and East Oweinat projects.

Laws relating to the conduct of foreign companies doing business in Egypt have been introduced. These include anti-dumping laws; regulations relating to intellectual

7

copyright, patents; the sale of goods and public tenders; and arbitration mechanisms for resolving disputes.

Law 4 of 1994, the Law for the Environment, was a step towards bringing Egypt into line with the internationally accepted standards discussed at the conference on the environment in Rio de Janeiro. The law was designed to protect the land, and in particular the coast line; it also makes provision for the protection of individuals in the workplace and aims to clean up the atmosphere in the urban areas of the country.

Taxation Laws

- Law 157 of 1981 regulates the taxes on corporate profits.

- Law 147 of 1984 regulates the duty for development.

- Law 159 offers tax holidays for certain enterprises.

- Law 54 of 1975 regulates tax exemption for private insurance funds.

- Law 187 of 1993 regulates personal taxation.

- Law 11 applies a general sales tax (likely to be replaced by VAT).

- The unified income tax law of 1994 regulates income.

Egypt has a double taxation agreement with the UK which has been in force since 1977. Customs duties and import regulations are in a state of flux as Egypt comes to terms with GATT. Patents, trademarks and copyright issues are covered by various laws. These too are under scrutiny.

Practicalities of opening an office

From a practical point of view, getting established in Egypt is not difficult. Estate agents will be able to locate offices in various parts of Cairo or the major cities of the country. For many years companies used converted apartments as offices, but it is now recognised that modern companies require purpose built facilities. Large multinationals have started to build corporate headquarters in Cairo or in one of the satellite cities. Government agencies have tended to remain in their old premises, although significant efforts are being made to establish office units in modern surroundings.

Office location

The location of an office is clearly important, with easy access to the airport and ring road being particularly significant. Is it possible for customers and clients to park near the office? This is important although most Egyptians will have a driver who will drop and collect them. Some areas are more suited to business operations than others: some are served better by terrestrial telephone lines; television or radio signals are poor in others; some districts are situated much more conveniently for residential areas and schools.

The main expatriate residential areas

Maadi is especially suited to oil companies, Americans (American School), British with young children (British junior school) and expatriates looking for a western atmosphere to live in.

Heliopolis is near the airport and the roads to Sinai and the Suez Canal zones. It is a pleasant clean location (the President lives here) and is near several British and American schools.

Zamalek is located on Gezirah island in the Nile. The former commercial heart of Egypt, it is a pleasant and convenient place to live and work in the centre of the city. The original British school is located there.

Mohandaseen and *Dokki* are central for living and working and generally popular areas for an office. Built by engineers for engineers they lack the character of other locations.

Office rents will usually be quoted in US dollars, especially for the better properties and for foreigners. Landlords will often suggest payment to their wife'saccount – this is presumably to assist with their annual accounting procedures. A three-bedroom flat with about 200 square metres of floorspace could cost from $1,000 US dollars per month. There are a few serviced offices offering full facilities immediately: secretarial services, couriers, telephones, photocopiers etc. ISS is one such company, which can provide purpose built serviced offices of a high standard in Heliopolis.

ISS: ❑ Tel & fax: (02) 2912218.

7

Communications

The Internet and e-mail are widely available. Although the two mobile phone networks still do not cover the whole country, they are generally satisfactory in the major cities and the GSM system has been incorporated into Egypt's mobile system allowing travellers to Egypt to use their own mobile phones. Telephone boxes are widespread in Cairo. Fax machines are widely used all over Egypt.

Telecoms

Obtaining a telephone line can still be difficult. Even in Cairo there are pockets in the city where immediate access to terrestrial lines is not possible. In Egypt local lines are generally available, while international numbers can be more difficult to access. However, things have improved since the eighties, when it was not uncommon to have to wait several years for a line. Local calls are very cheap and therefore the use of e-mail and cc-mail (with a local number) is preferable to the use of international telephone calls or faxed messages.

7

International terrestrial and satellite television has recently become available in Egypt including major networks and channels in most languages. Egypt has launched communications satellites to improve the standard and availability of its own television broadcasting.

Post

The postal system in Egypt remains unsatisfactory; delivery cannot be guaranteed either locally or internationally. Most companies use their own messengers or drivers to deliver mail within Egypt and international couriers deliver mail throughout the country and overseas.

Staff

Rates of pay in Egypt are low by European and American standards. Large numbers of staff are employed in offices and factories, even in the private sector – the number of tea boys and drivers that companies employ will usually astonish a newcomer to the country.

Salaries

Staff are generally employed on a monthly salary, starting at about LE400 for a driver or tea boy going to LE1,500 for a secretary and perhaps LE3,000 for a reasonable accountant. Benefits must include social insurance; bonuses and transport allowance may also be paid.

Taxes and other salary deductions must be made and remitted regularly to the authorities.

There are situations vacant columns in the local Arabic papers, which will print an advertisement in any language – an English advertisement should cut out applications from individuals who don't speak the language.

In Egypt there is a good pool of potential local employees. Egyptians will have gone to university and may be highly qualified. As in other countries it has become more difficult for graduates to find employment. Formerly, graduates were guaranteed employment in government offices, but this privilege has been abolished so it is now common to find a graduate of business studies, for example, driving a taxi around Cairo.

Recruiting locally

Working Hours
Working hours in Egypt are haphazard and even vary during the year. The weekend is generally Friday. Shops are mostly open on Fridays and close on Sundays, although supermarkets are open seven days a week. Many offices work on Saturdays, although this does not include ministries, embassies and banks.

7

Offices tend to open at 0830 in the morning, especially in the more modern private industries, and close at approximately 1700. The old practice of starting late, breaking for a siesta and working until late in the evening is still observed by some offices but is becoming less popular. Government offices usually close at 1430, and are closed on Thursday and Friday.

Hours of business

There is a rush hour in the morning from about 0730 to 0930 and then another in the afternoon from about 1400 until 1800. During the school year (September to June), traffic in Cairo is considerably worse. In the summer when the schools are closed many Cairenes take a long vacation and traffic in Cairo is quite reasonable during the day. In Alexandria, a popular resort, it becomes dreadful.

Starting up
When coming to Egypt a foreign company should always retain its independence and avoid becoming reliant upon a local organisation or agent for support. However

financially attractive it might seem to be while negotiating a deal, resist the temptation of any offers of support that are not strictly necessary. Allow foreign staff to choose their own accommodation, make their own transport arrangements, buy cars and appoint drivers. All-inclusive salary packages for foreign staff make administration much more straightforward and avoid misunderstandings.

Expatriate staff will soon become acquainted with the social scene in the country. Those with sporting interests and with children at one of the many international schools will soon meet other expatriates. There are many social and sporting organisations in Egypt allowing individuals to pursue their own interests, ranging from archaeology to rugby. Business groups also offer executives the opportunity to discuss problems that arise while working in Egypt. Such groups as the American Chamber or the British Egyptian Business Association are there to assist with information and introductions.

7

8

Cairo

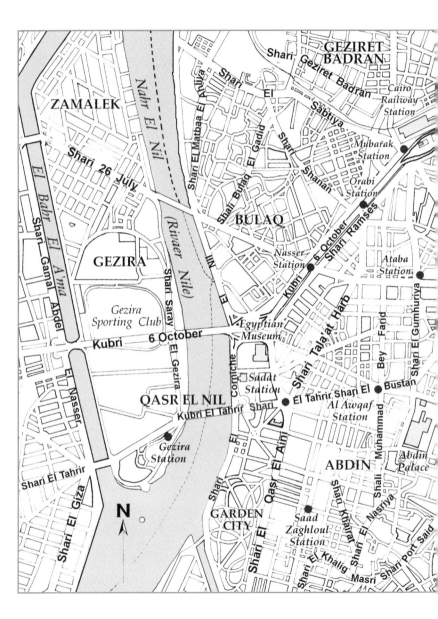

Cairo

Cairo

Cairo is the commercial and political capital of Egypt and is the most important academic religious centre of the Muslim world. The first site for the capital, al-Fustat, was located just south of the existing city and the medieval Muslim city was centred on the area occupied today by Khan el Khalili. Cairo, known to Egyptians as the 'Mother of the World', is a city where poor mingle with rich, Christians with Muslims, refugees from Africa with expatriates from the west; where Mercedes jostle for space with donkeys and carts in the narrow streets and where the mosque minarets dwarf the lurid hand-painted hoardings for the cinemas.

Cairo is situated on either side of the River Nile just before the river divides into smaller channels for its passage through the fertile agricultural areas of the Delta to the Mediterranean Sea. The Nile itself has for centuries acted as the primary means of access to Upper Egypt and is still today an important waterway. A common sight are the river barges moving up and down the river and the sailing *feluccas,* so much a symbol of Egypt. The river buses crossing back and forth mix with floating restaurants, oarsmen from the rowing clubs, waterskiers and the dinghy sailors.

Cairo is a crossroads for land transport north and south; Egypt links Europe, Africa and Asia. The city has for many centuries been a destination for the camel trains from central and southern Africa. Herds of camels are still driven up from Sudan to the markets in Cairo. It is still a frequent sight to see these herds, with their nomadic herdsmen from Sudan swathed in white, fighting their way through the evening rush hour in the city, on their way to market. Caravanserais, where traders arriving in the city could sell their wares, rest above the shop and stable their camels nearby, can still be seen.

Areas of Cairo: Where to Live

Maadi is a suburb to the south of Cairo located on the River Nile. Local entrepreneurs developed Maadi at the beginning of the 20th century for foreign residents and Egyptian gentry. It is adjacent to the rail track which has recently been adapted to accommodate the new Metro

8

Maadi

trains connecting Maadi to central Cairo and beyond. Some areas of Maadi have retained their colonial past with Raj-style bungalows, Swiss chalets and large mansions, some complete with gardens which would not look out of place in an English village. The village of Helwan, just to the south of Maadi, was once known as Helwan-les-Bains and was a health resort for Europeans. Nasser transformed this area into an industrial zone with steel mills, cement works and assembly plants.

Nowadays Maadi has other attractions. The Victoria College sports grounds offer facilities for activities as diverse as rugby and baseball. There is a large American school, a smaller British school and European-style supermarkets and fast-food outlets.

Heliopolis to the north of Cairo is not on the Nile but is near the airport. Perhaps because the President resides there, it is a clean, tidy, attractive suburb. The Belgian Baron Empain laid out the area at the end of the 19th century and his palace, modelled on a Hindu temple, can be seen adjacent to the current airport road. Empain designed Heliopolis with tree-lined boulevards and a system of trams radiating from his palace. These boulevards exist today with the trams still running along the centre. The unusual architecture of the shopping area of Heliopolis was chosen for filming some scenes for the British television series set in Egypt, *Fortunes of War*. Heliopolis is convenient for the new ring road and the facilities at New Cairo.

Zamalek, located in central Cairo on Gezirah island was *the* place to live early in the 20th century. The Khedive Ismail started the fashion when he built a palace for the visiting Empress Eugenie of France at the time of the opening of the Suez Canal. The palace was complete with gardens that covered a large part of the island and encouraged development; it is now a Marriot hotel. The once exclusive but now rather faded Gezirah Sporting Club still has a wide range of activities on offer, including polo, horse racing, croquet, swimming, tennis, squash, athletics, gymnastics and golf, together with social and restaurant facilities.

There are still a few villas on the island, although most of these are occupied by embassies or their staff. The older apartment buildings offer pleasant accommodation but

Heliopolis

8

Zamalek

are disadvantaged by narrow streets and limited parking. Only in the last decade have buildings been erected with sufficient car parking for the residents.

The British International School on the island is considering moving from its cramped and ancient buildings to new premises on the outskirts of the city in New Cairo. The unusual Anglican Cathedral, relocated in the sixties to avoid the 6th October highway, hides between towering blocks of apartments and the Marriot hotel.

Mohandaseen and Dokki are on the west bank of the Nile. There are some attractive parts based around tree-lined squares which offer cheaper accommodation for those people who need to live close to the centre of Cairo and their offices. A modern sporting club in the centre of this area, known as the Shooting Club, has extensive facilities.

Mohandaseen

Dokki

Giza offers special attractions to those looking for something different. Luxury on the Nile or horse riding at the Pyramids are more affordable in these areas. Although the western part of Giza by the Pyramids is now connected to Cairo by the new ring road, access to the centre by road is still slow. New housing developments, together with the 26th July Corridor and a proposed extension to the existing Metro mean that parts of Giza are beginning to offer the suburban commuting lifestyle to the growing population.

8

Giza

Garden City was once one of the smart places to live. Laid out with curved narrow tree-lined roads, the area has fallen into decay with traffic congestion and parking problems. Some old villas with their large gardens can still be seen; old blocks of majestic apartments with marble and stone floors, high ceilings and graceful windows still remain. However, much of the area was wrecked during the fifties and sixties. Few foreigners can be found in this part of town, although it is almost adjacent to the city centre.

Garden City

New Cairo or *Kattameia, Shorook* and *Sheik Ziad City* are the new suburbs located near the ring road. Schools and universities are relocating to Kattameia and two international-standard golf courses have been built. For the price of an apartment in the centre of the city a family can enjoy a villa with swimming pool and garden.

New suburbs

Education is nearby, the airport is within easy reach, there is good access to the coastal resorts and the way of life is generally healthier and more pleasant than in town, although these areas still lack character and access to central Cairo is not that easy.

Agouza, Shoubra, Imbaba, Bab el Louk and the two areas known as Beaulac (the beautiful lakes have long since gone) are not areas where an expatriate might live, nor is Kit Kat Square (named after an earlier nightclub). Roxy (named after the cinema), a suburb of Heliopolis, might be suitable as might Beverly Hills when it is finished. An alternative for those wishing to live a less conventional life might be an apartment on one of the old house boats moored on the river. While these are becoming quite fashionable, Imbaba, where they are moored, is definitely not.

How to Get About

The Metro is the first underground railway system in Africa, and is being extended from its early routes on the east bank of the river to encompass more and more of the city on both sides of the Nile. The Metro uses modern rolling stock and runs quietly on its new track.

Walking around Cairo, particularly the old city, is perhaps the best way to get a feel for the place but does have its problems, the principal one being exactly where to walk. If you walk on the pavement or sidewalk you will find innumerable obstacles to your progress, ranging from parked cars, uneven surfaces and missing manhole covers to street vendors.

Valet parking on every street

Anywhere cars can be parked, a self appointed attendant patrols. He will, for regular generous clients, find a place in the crowded streets. Cars are parked bumper-to-bumper with their brakes off so the attendant can shunt the cars to maximise available spaces Some streets allow parking on one side only, but there are no signs or attendants to clarify this. Only when the car is ticketed, clamped or – worse – towed away, will this be known. Double parking is common, again cars will be shunted to allow others to come and go.

8

On the road...

Most Cairo residents have seen three camels in the back of a small pick-up truck, looking around enquiringly, unaware that their probable destination is the butcher. The same pick-up will be the vehicle used by the family for a Friday outing, Children, chattels, and wives are consigned to the back, while brothers and sons travel in luxury in the front with the driver, The numbers game is popular with expatriates: the maximum number on a motorbike – 5; maximum in the front of a taxi – 4 (one passenger has his right arm around the driver); maximum on a bus – 10 (on the bus roof); maximum in a bus - beyond counting.

Although in Saudi Arabia women are still not allowed to drive, in Cairo the sight of mothers driving their children to school during term time is common.

Vehicles in Egypt were generally old until factories were built in the country in the late 1980s. Now the streets of Cairo are full of Egyptian-produced BMWs, Mercedes, Opels, Jeeps and Chryslers.

8

Cairo residents who choose to use their own cars but who do not have the luxury of a driver face the twin perils of driving and parking. There are a few multi-story car parks and some parking places available at the major hotels but the most common if not the preferred option is the street. Projects to encourage investors and businessmen to build and operate car parks throughout the city are being promoted by the two governates responsible for the city.

Road Safety

Serious efforts are being made in Egypt to reduce fatalities on the roads, especially in remote areas. Government ambulance stations are on main routes throughout the country, including Sinai. The advent of mobile phones will enable emergencies to be reported quickly. Still the advice from most people in the country, including the British Embassy, is not to travel on the roads outside Cairo or the major cities at night.

Hotels and Restaurants

There is a large variety of accommodation in Egypt, ranging from five-star hotels to youth hostels. Listed below are some of the hotels favoured by business travellers in Egypt, together with comments upon services and facilities

Hotels

Central Cairo

These hotels are convenient for most major offices and embassies. They offer access to all parts of the city and are those most consistently used by business travellers.

Cairo Sheraton ★★★★– on the west bank of the Nile in Giza. It is a large hotel offering the usual business facilities and is much used by Arabs from the Gulf and Saudi Arabia. It is capable of hosting small exhibitions and seminars. Some rooms overlook the Nile and others offer a view of the Pyramids on a clear day. The hotel is one of the largest and has several restaurants to choose from, although none actually on the river. The hotel is keen to encourage corporate travellers and offers a health club and a small rooftop swimming pool.
❏ Tel: (02) 3369700/800; fax: (02) 3364601
Website: [www.sheratonaficamideast.com]
E-mail: [Csher@rite.com]

Conrad Hilton – on the east bank of the Nile a little north of the city centre and the most recent addition to Cairo's hotels. It currently offers the most up to date facilities for the business traveller and is adjacent to the World Trade Centre, where many significant offices and the Australian Embassy are located. Some of the best shops in Cairo are located in the Centre's shopping mall.
❏ Tel: (02) 5808000; fax: (02) 5808080
E-mail: [conrad@intouch.com]

Gezirah Sheraton – on the southern tip of Gezirah Island near the smart residential area of Zamalek. The hotel is a round tower and all rooms have magnificent views of the city and the river. It has several riverside restaurants and a small health club and pool. Executive floors are a little more expensive and have recently been refurbished.
❏ Tel: (02) 737 3737; fax: (02) 736 3640
Website: [www.sheratonaficamideast.com]
E-mail: [Gzsher@rite.com]

8

The Golden Tulip Flamenco ★★★★★ – in the heart of Zamalek on Gezirah Island. A small, friendly and less expensive hotel suitable for long stays and those on a medium budget. Rooms overlook the Nile and the Pyramids.
❑ Tel: (02) 3400815/6; fax: (02) 3400819
E-mail: [Bcflamenco@rite.com]

Helnan Shepherd ★★★★★– in Garden City very close to the British and American embassies. Much used by tourists, this local chain offers a cheaper alternative to the major international hotels. The Helnan group operate throughout Egypt. The hotel has a choice of restaurants.
❑ Tel: (02) 3553800/900; fax: (02) 3557284
E-mail: [Reshs@helnan.com]

Hilton Residence – in the World Trade Centre. Offers furnished serviced apartments and is often used by short-term expatriate visitors who prefer some independence.
❑ Tel: (02) 5802000; fax: (02) 5790577

Le Meridien Cairo ★★★★★– on the northern tip of Roda Island in Garden City near the British and American embassies. It has one of the finest sites for any hotel in Cairo – right on the Nile. All rooms are large and have magnificent Nile views. There are good restaurants and Nile side terraced areas for relaxation. The current building was one of the first business hotels to be built in Cairo and is undergoing major renovation and extension. In the year 2000 it is expected that the new 760 bedroom extension will be operating and the old building converted to luxury suites. The hotel offers good business services.
❑ Tel: (02) 3621717; fax: (02) 3621927
E-mail: [Mercaic@internetegypt.com]

Marriott ★★★★★– in Zamalek on Gezirah Island. Its public areas were built by the Khedive Ismail as a palace for the Empress Eugénie of France at the time of the opening of the Suez Canal. The guest wings were added in the 1960s and the hotel opened. It has good sporting facilities in its large garden and a number of good restaurants, including a floating dining area with live entertainment. Used by business travellers and Gulf visitors alike.
❑ Tel: (02) 3408888; fax: (02) 3406667
Website: [www.marriotthotels.com/CAIEG]
E-mail: [Marriott@link.com.eg]

8

Nile Hilton ★★★★★– the first modern hotel to be built in Egypt, situated in the very centre of Cairo off Tahrir Square, adjacent to the Egyptian Museum. The rooms are large and offer good views over the city and the river. It is very conveniently located for most offices and embassies. Good formal and informal restaurants. There is a health club, squash and tennis courts and a large heated outdoor swimming pool in the gardens. The hotel is much favoured by businessmen and tourists and is often fully booked.
❏ Tel: (02) 5780444/666; fax: (02) 5780475/476

Pyramisa ★★★★★– a tourist class hotel in Giza near the river. It does however have facilities for business travellers and can offer large rooms for those requiring more space.
❏ Tel: (02) 3367000/8000; fax: (02) 3605347

President Hotel – a small hotel in Zamalek especially suitable for those business travellers on a tighter budget.
❏ Tel: (02) 3400718/0652; fax: (02) 3411752

Ramses Hilton ★★★★★– another in the Hilton chain located just up from the Nile Hilton on the river. Favoured by tourists, business travellers and some long stay guests. It has good facilities and restaurants.
❏ Tel: (02) 5758000/5744000; fax: (02) 5757152
e-mail [Rhinet@intouch.com].

Semiramis Intercontinental ★★★★★– a large hotel in Garden City, on the Nile just off Tahrir Square. It is currently one of the largest business hotels in Cairo and much used by Gulf Arabs and travellers from Saudi Arabia. It has a good roof top pool and many restaurants. Convenient for business travellers.
❏ Tel: (02) 3557171; fax: (02) 3561320
E-mail: [Cairo@interconti.com]

Four Seasons Hotel - in Giza next to the zoo. This hotel is part of the First Residence complex and will be the best in Cairo offering a full international five star service. Although the location is not very convenient for central Cairo it is located near some major offices and organisations and is next door to the French Embassy. See on its website: [www.fourseasons.com]

Four Seasons Hotel – in Garden City. Construction started in 1999.

8

Hotels like the *Windsor* and *Safir* offer cheap reasonable accommodation in the centre of Cairo.

Heliopolis

Very close to the airport and nearer the satellite cities of 10th Ramadan and New Cairo, and the industrial areas to the north of Cairo. These hotels are also convenient for the Delta and the roads to Ismailia, Suez and Sinai. They are located near the new Cairo ring road, which provides easy access to the suburb of Maadi, the roads to Alexandria and routes to Upper Egypt.

Baron Hotel – small Egyptian-run budget hotel favoured by visiting business travellers on a medium budget. Good business services and restaurants in a pleasant area.
❏ Tel: (02) 2915757/2467; fax: (02) 2907077

Meridien Heliopolis ★★★★★– medium sized business hotel offering good simple facilities.
❏ Tel: (02) 2905055/1819; fax: (02) 4172492

Movenpick Hotel – within walking distance of the airport, especially suitable for transit travellers. Good service and food from this Swiss based operator. The hotel has a swimming pool and health club.
❏ Tel: (02) 2470077/2919400; fax: (02) 4180761
E-mail: [e-mail@movenpickhel.com.eg]

Novotel ★★★★– very near the airport and especially suitable for transit passengers.
❏ Tel: (02) 2918520; fax: (02) 2914794

Sheraton Heliopolis – the most recent addition to the Sheraton hotels in Cairo. It is famous for its atrium and the food outlets located around it. Excellent sporting and business facilities. The hotel is a low rise building near the airport on the main airport road.
❏ Tel: (02) 2677730/40; fax: (02) 6678170
Website: [www.sheratonafricamideast.com].

Sonesta Hotel – in Nasr City, half way between the airport and the city centre. Popular with business visitors.
❏ Tel: (02) 2628111/2617100; fax: (02) 2635731
e-mail: [sonbc@brainy1.ie-eg.com].

Swissotel Cairo el Salam ★★★★★– to the west of Heliopolis in large grounds. The hotel offers good food

8

and sporting facilities and is particularly convenient for the Ismailia Road and 10th Ramadan city.
❏ Tel: (02) 2974000/6000; fax: (02) 2976037

Pyramids Area

Hotels in this area are near the satellite cities of 6th October and Sheikh Ziad and the desert road to Alexandria. Access to the rest of Cairo is by the ring road and other radial corridors. These hotels are mostly used by tourists although they do offer business facilities.

Mena House Hotel ★★★★★– probably the most famous in this area. The hotel public areas were formerly a royal hunting lodge and hosted wartime meetings between Churchill and Roosevelt. It is immediately adjacent to the Giza Pyramid plateau. The guest-rooms were added in the sixties, together with the other guest facilities. The hotel is operated by the Indian Oberoi group and has probably the best Indian restaurant in Cairo.
❏ Tel: (02) 3833444/222; fax: (02) 3837777
E-mail: [Obmhobc@oberoi.com.eg]

Meridien Pyramids ★★★★★– large tourist hotel.
❏ Tel: (02) 3830772; fax: (02) 3831730

Movenpick Pyramids – friendly Swiss run hotel. Good sporting facilities.
❏ Tel: (02) 3852555/666; fax: (02) 3835006.

The Siag and *The Sofitel* ★★★★★– hotels offer good local alternatives for travellers.

Maadi

For those dealing with some of the major oil and gas companies in Maadi, a suburb to the south of Cairo, there is only one hotel in the area and that is the:

Sofitel Maadi Towers ★★★★★– on the Nile. Reasonable facilities for business and tourist travellers. Maadi, one of the main areas for resident expatriates, has many shops and restaurants.
❏ Tel: (02) 5260601; fax: (02) 5261133

Restaurants
The business traveller is most likely to eat in his or her hotel, where most of the international-style restaurants of an acceptable standard are located. It would,

8

however, be a shame to ignore completely the local cuisine.

Drinking alcohol in Egypt is not a problem. Egypt brews acceptable beer, which is available in draft, canned or bottled form. In 1999 Egypt started to produce wine under a privatisation agreement with foreign expertise and the old local wineries. These new wines are quite drinkable. Local spirits should not be drunk. Serious health problems and even deaths have arisen from consumption of local spirits.

Most restaurants and hotels now serve bottled water. Tap water can be very heavily chlorinated in Cairo, making it unpleasant to drink, but *possibly* safe. Major hotels and cruise ships now have water purifiers for their domestic systems.

Restaurants in Cairo
Formal restaurants

The following restaurants offer international cuisine and are suitable venues for formal dinners. If business discussions are planned, avoid live music which tends to be loud.

8

Champollion at the Meridien, Cairo.
❑ Tel: (02) 3621717

Rumours at the Gezirah Sheraton. Overlooks the Nile and has regular live music.
❑ Tel: (02) 3411333

Villa D'este at the Conrad Hilton.
❑ Tel: (02) 5799399

Grill Room at the Semiramis Intercontinental.
❑ Tel: (02) 3557171

Belvedere at the Nile Hilton. Has a outside rooftop bar adjacent to the restaurant overlooking the Nile.
❑ Tel: (02) 5780444

Chinois at the Heliopolis Sheraton. Far Eastern food. Interesting atrium area with six other café-type outlets.
❑ Tel: (02) 2677730

Les Trefles is opposite the World Trade Centre and the Conrad Hilton and is on the river.
❑ Tel: (02) 5796511

Aladdin at the Giza Sheraton is for those who like Lebanese food and live oriental music.
❏ Tel: (02) 3369700

Le Chateau in Giza overlooking the Nile. Swiss run.
❏ Tel: (02) 3485321

Marco Polo at the Meridien Heliopolis.
❏ Tel: (02) 2905055

The Moghul Room at the Mena House, by the Pyramids. Small restaurant which serves very good Indian food.
❏ Tel: (02) 3833222

JW's Steakhouse at the Marriott Zamalek.
❏ Tel: (02) 2294661

Le Steak located on a large boat, permanently moored near the Marriott Hotel. There are also several other good restaurants on the boat.
❏ Tel: (02) 3406730

Piano Bar at the World Trade Centre.
❏ Tel: (02) 5749556

Silk Road – oriental restaurant at the Swisshotel Cairo el Salaam Hotel in Heliopolis.
❏ Tel: (02) 2974000

Informal or moderately-priced Restaurants
The major hotels have several restaurants including a 'coffee shop'.

Arabesque Egyptian food served in a quiet surroundings.
❏ Tel: (02) 5747898

The Regent at the Ramses Hilton serves Chinese food.
❏ Tel: (02) 5758000

Fish Market On a boat at Giza – for those who like fresh fish, chosen and cooked to order. It is located on the same boat as the much advertised *TGI Friday*.
❏ Tel: (02) 5709690

La Mamma Italian food at the Cairo Sheraton.
❏ Tel: (02) 3369700

Bua Khao Thai restaurants in Maadi and at the Nile Hilton food court annex. Very popular.
❏ Tel: (02) 3580126

Swiss Chalet Chain which offers very good simple food in pleasant surroundings in Giza, Maadi, downtown and Heliopolis – which has a garden bar attached.
❏ Tel: (02) 3518328

Chopsticks in Mohandaseen and Maadi offers Singaporean/Chinese food.
❏ Tel: (02) 3048567

Taj Mahal is an Indian restaurant in Mohandaseen.
❏ Tel: (02) 3025669

Da Mario The Italian restaurant at the Nile Hilton is worth a visit and has more than just pizza and pasta.
❏ Tel: (02) 5780444

Four Corners restaurants include *Justine* (see above) and *La Piazza* (Italian), *Chin Chin* (Chinese) and an American restaurant with pop videos playing.
❏ Tel: (02) 3412961

Roy's Country Kitchen at the Marriott Hotel is open 24 hours a day and serves American food. Popular place to read and eat on your own.
❏ Tel: (02) 3394661

Fast Food Outlets
Cairo has many fast food outlets, including *McDonalds, Wimpy, Pizza Hut, Kentucky Fried Chicken* and *Domino's Pizza*. There are also locally-owned eateries in this style, including *Deals, Zinc, Fat Black Pussycat* and *Aubergines*. They all offer good food in a lively atmosphere often with live music. The *Hard Rock Café* is open in Sharm el Sheikh and Cairo, *TGI Friday* is opening several outlets and *Planet Hollywood* will soon open.

Floating Restaurants and Egyptian Food
No trip to Cairo is complete without dining on one of the floating restaurants on the Nile. The Marriott has the *Nile Maxim*. The *Pharaohs* boat starts at Giza and the *Nile Crystal* boats start from Maadi. These boats and several others offer a buffet dinner with a belly dancer, a whirling dervish and an Egyptian band. The trip lasts about two hours.

Felfella serves cheap local food in a café-style surroundings. They have several outlets in Cairo. Their restaurant in Hurghada overlooks the sea.

8

Andreas is a garden restaurant near the Pyramids and Maadi. A popular family venue.

Restaurants outside Cairo

Sharm el Sheikh has many good restaurants. Many of them also offer entertainment. For those travellers staying for some time and who may like a change there is a good Indian restaurant at the Sofitel and a branch of *Bua Khao* in the New Sharm Hotel. The *Star of Sinai* restaurant is in a small warehouse in the shopping area and serves fish of the day very cheaply – no menu.

Alexandria also has many restaurants, although not as many up to the international standards found in Cairo, nor offering the same variety of food. It is worth remembering that Alex is a summer holiday resort for the people of Cairo. As a coastal town, Alexandria has also become known for the quality of its fish restaurants. Excellent marine fare can be found at the *Fish Market* (owned by the similar outlet in Cairo) which overlooks the harbour, *Samakmak* a small café and the *Sea Gull* located in a large strange building to the west of the port. For the serious eaters of fresh fish and those who are prepared to eat in a large restaurant with few refinements, the *Zephyrion* at Abu Kir, to the East of the city, is a must.

Night Clubs and Casinos

The big hotels have casinos, patronised largely by wealthy Arabs. Tourists and business travellers too are frequently to be seen at the tables late into the night or early morning.

Most of the large hotels also have a nightclub. These clubs offer the usual expensive drinks, belly dancers, loud music and late night entertainment for those who have the time and money. The Pyramids Road and its old clubs is probably best avoided except by the hardened international clubbers. Separate night clubs and hotel casinos are also opening at the coastal resorts.

Recreations for the resident expatriate

A very popular pastime with expatriates is horse riding. While there are no specific clubs there are many stables where horses can be hired. Regular riders can lease a horse for the duration of their stay, but take on the responsibility of ensuring that the horse is looked

8

after correctly. Horse riding in the desert near the Giza Pyramids is an excellent way to draw fresh air into the lungs after the pollution of Cairo.

The Gezirah Sporting Club

For many decades this oasis in the centre of Cairo has occupied a large proportion of Gezirah Island in the Nile. It was once the focal point for the social scene in Egypt. During the Second World War, officers of the allied armies congregated here for their sport and recreation, mixing with the numerous foreign residents and the elite of Egyptian society. To be a member of "The Club" was a must.

A large number of people still use the club, but membership is limited to existing Egyptian members, their families and a few expatriates. The Club is less now of a social than a sporting centre. A running track occupies the site of the cricket pitch, but the old benches in the shade which surround the track, still seem ideal for watching the leather and the willow.

There are football pitches and a golf course now reduced to nine holes. Horse racing takes place in the winter and polo in the spring: fine horses are stabled in some style in the far corner of the club. The swimming pool is reminiscent of the old council Lidos in England.

8

Clubs, associations and sports

- British Community Association. (Mohandaseen and Heliopolis). Social pub-like atmosphere. BCA runs the annual Queen's Birthday Ball (QBB), the last big social event of the season before expatriates depart for their summer leave.

- Women's Association.

- Community Service Association. (Maadi) Helps new residents settle in. Offers orientation, advice and support.

- British Council. (Agouza, Heliopolis, also Alexandria) Runs various courses, including Arabic and IT. Has a good library with books, video and music cassettes.

- Hibernian Society.
- Scottish Country Dancing. Annual St Andrew's Night Ball and regular practice.
- Cairo Players, Amateur dramatics.
- Choral Society. Gives ambitious concerts.
- Hash House Harriers. Fun runs every Friday. There are now two clubs in Cairo.
- British Golf Society. Holds regular competitions and has an annual tournament at one of the courses away from Cairo. There are now six major courses around Cairo and others in Alexandria, Sharm el Sheikh, Hurghada and other resorts.
- Egyptian Exploration Society. Tours led by leading archaeologists.
- Alcoholics Anonymous.
- Befrienders. Like Samaritans.
- Swimming clubs. Facilities at all the major hotels and also some country clubs.
- Squash. Some hotels and the Gezirah Club.
- Cairo Rugby Club. Social and active players welcomed. Organisers of the annual raft race on the Nile.
- Baseball, softball and little league. American sports club in Maadi.
- British Sub Aqua Club. Meets regularly in Cairo. There are many diving schools in the Red Sea resorts offering PADDY qualifications.
- Darts league.
- Windsurfing. Some areas of the Bitter Lakes on the Suez Canal are ideal for learners, while the west coast of Sinai offers professional conditions for the experts.
- Water Skiing. Apart from the resorts, skiing is also possible on the Nile in Cairo.
- Bridge at the BCA and other local groups.
- Tree Lovers' association.
- Rowing club – pairs to eights on the river.

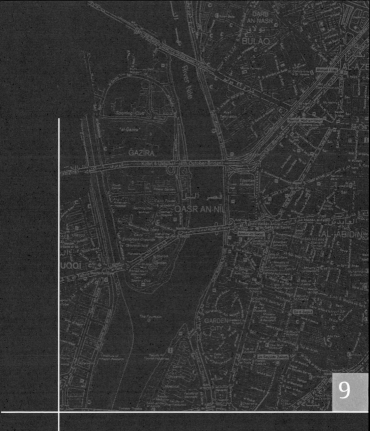

9

other cities

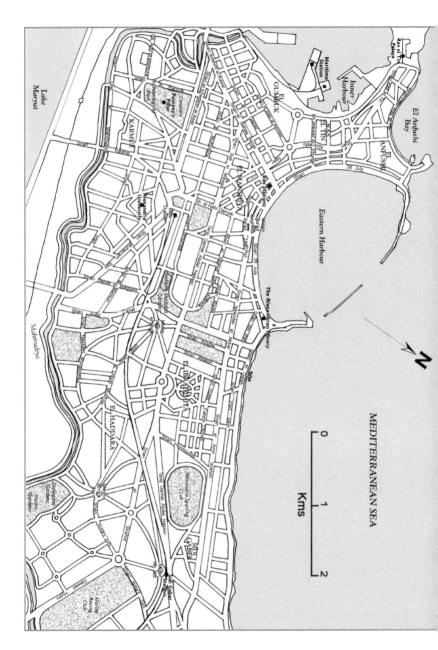

Alexandria

Alexandria and Environs

Most business travellers will probably venture no further than Cairo. However, executives with a day to spare should consider visiting Alexandria, through which much of Egypt's trade passes.

When Alexander the Great conquered Egypt more than two thousand years ago, he built a new capital on the Mediterranean Sea. Alexander's general Ptolemy and his successors as rulers of Egypt made Alexandria a centre of intellectual excellence. Euclid the inventor of geometry, and Eratosthenes, who calculated the dimensions of the earth, lived in Alexandria during this period. The lighthouse or Pharos, one of the seven wonders of the ancient world, guided shipping into port and the city's library became the most important in the world.

History

The importance of Alexandria declined during the Roman period but it was still the most important city in Egypt when, in the seventh century, the country was conquered by the Muslim Arabs. Amr ibn al-As, the Arab general, described the city as having 4,000 palaces, numerous public baths and theatres but despite this decided to establish his capital, *al Fustat*, further south near present-day Cairo. For over a thousand years Alexandria was a backwater so that when Napoleon arrived in 1778 there was little left of its former glory and few inhabitants.

9

The revival of Alexandria began under Mohammed Ali's energetic and modernising rule in the early nineteenth century The city flourished as a centre of Mediterranean trade and Levantine culture. This cosmopolitan atmosphere continued until President Nasser expelled British and French citizens and nationalised foreign industries following the Suez crisis of 1956. The literary city of Cavafy, Durrell and Forster declined; the glamour all but disappeared, with today only the occasional Greek, French or Italian name above a shop or café remaining to hint at what the city once was.

The climate in Alexandria is very different to other cities in Egypt. The cool breeze from the sea makes it pleasant, albeit humid, in the summer. Winter is like any European Mediterranean coastal city, with rain and cold winds driving in from the sea. Until the 1952 revolution the Royal court moved from Cairo to Alexandria for the

Climate

summer months. Ambassadors, government officials, domestic staff and families followed so that each summer a large part of Cairo moved north.

The tradition of spending the summer in Alexandria continues, when the population of the city increases by fifty per cent to 6 million. To the west of the city a holiday town of Agami has developed, and the apartment blocks now straggle along the coast beyond El Alamein towards the Libyan border.

In Alexandria itself there have been radical recent improvements: in 1998 the new governor restored the Corniche and removed concrete beach huts from the beaches. He moved the city airport to the suburbs at Borg al Arab, continued with the improvements to the water and sewerage systems (with support from USAID) and started a ring road to alleviate traffic congestion.

The **main port** for Egypt is situated between Alexandria and Agami; it is capable of handling containers and bulk cargoes. The old shipyard, adjacent to the port, expanded considerably with Russian support after it was nationalised, and continues to be state owned. Private port initiatives in Egypt and in other countries around the Mediterranean have undermined Alexandria's competitiveness as a centre of ship building and repair. The development within Egypt of Damietta port and the proposed new hub container terminal at Port Said will further erode the position of the port of Alexandria.

Hotels

The city is spread out along twenty-two kilometres of sea front. Business hotels are few, and are generally at the *Montaza*

Helnan Palestine ★★★★★– superb position on the sea. Adequate facilities.
❏ Tel: (03) 5474033; fax: (03) 5473378
E-mail: [RESHP@helnan.com]

Ramada Renaissance – modern hotel on the sea front.
❏ Tel: (03) 5490935; fax: (03) 5497690

Sheraton – modern hotel on the sea front.
❏ Tel: (03) 5480550; fax: (03) 5401331

9

Salamlek Hotel – a very small exclusive hotel with each bedroom in its own individual style. A little more expensive than the chain hotels it can offer very large luxurious suites sufficient to hold small receptions. The most luxurious accommodation in Alexandria. Sister hotel to the San Giovanni.
❏ Tel: (03) 5477999; fax: (03) 5473585

Central Alexandria

Cecil Hotel – operated by the Sofitel chain, this hotel is probably the most famous in Alexandria with strong literary and wartime connections. It is a little faded now but has the best location for central Alexandria and is on the sea front.
❏ Tel: (03) 4837173; fax: (03) 4836401

Mercure Romance – also in central Alexandria. Offers good reasonably priced accommodation.
❏ Tel: (03) 5876429; fax: (03) 5870526

San Giovanni – the only hotel on the sea front actually on the sea side of the main road. Reasonably priced accommodation in pleasant surroundings.
❏ Tel: (03) 5467774/5; fax: (03) 5464408

The *Delta*, ★★★ *Lords Inn* and *Maamoura* hotels provide reasonable and cheaper accommodation.

Around Alexandria

Borg al Arab and *Amreya* are two of the main industrial areas around Alexandria. Borg al Arab is 50 kilometres to the west and Amreya 30 kilometres to the south. Pharmaceuticals, textiles, food and paint are manufactured here. A major modern steel works built with Japanese and British support is also in the region. Borg al Arab covers an area in excess of 200 square kilometres and has a population of half million working in some five hundred businesses. A light rail link is planned to transport workers from Alexandria to Borg al Arab. *Noubariya*, a smaller development, is 80 kilometres south of Alexandria. Occupying a tenth of the area of Borg al Arab, it is important due to its proximity to the agricultural industries and farms of the Delta.

New Damietta City is a small development near Damietta to the east of Alexandria. Apart from its importance as a port, Damietta is well known for its wood-working industries,

9

Borg al Arab
Amreya

New Damietta City

specialising in furniture and the fine **Mashrabya** window screens that were formerly fitted to so many fine buildings in Egypt.

One of the major problems arising from the volume of industry in and around Alexandria is the pollution of the sea and nearby lakes. Behind the city and preventing inland development are several lakes one of which, Lake Mariout, is so heavily polluted that it is the site of a number of international environmental aid projects. Fishermen however, still catch and eat the fish breeding within it.

Around Cairo

There are several new cities. Founded during the rule of President Anwar Sadat as overspill towns for Cairo, they have now acquired their own identity. The closest to Cairo and most developed, **6th October City**, has in turn developed its own satellite – **Sheikh Ziad City**.

6th October City is 40 kilometres west of Cairo on the Fayoum Road. It occupies an area of about 400 square kilometres and has been laid out to accommodate future developments. Major projects, such as a new media city (film and television studios and sets), a factory for photocopiers and the headquarter buildings for the mobile phone companies are located here. A theme park, golf course, hotel and convention centre is also under construction. In the city centre the local management committee have their offices, and a large sports and social club was opened some years ago. Hotels are planned in association with villa and apartment developments.

Sheikh Ziad City has a new hospital and technical university. The town council is proposing that the city should be entirely privately run – the first BOOT project of its kind in Egypt. Luxury villas and apartments are also under construction.

10th Ramadan City, 50 kilometres east of Cairo, occupies another 400 square kilometres of desert. It is one of the original satellites and the furthest from Cairo. Small and medium sized manufacturing industries have been operational here for some years. There are currently about five hundred factories and, because of its distance from Cairo, many of the workers now live locally.

Sadat City, 90 kilometres from Cairo on the Alexandria road, is one of the largest – 500 square kilometres – and

6th October City

9

Sheikh Ziad City

10th Ramadan City

best planned new cities. It is a residential and industrial town specialising in heavy industry, close to Mediterranean ports. Half a million people are now living in Sadat City.

15th May, Badr and **New Salheya** cities are small industrial developments with a variety of specialisations. Projects to stimulate local industries at Minya and Beni Suef have been initiated in the Nile Valley south of Cairo which has traditionally relied upon agriculture.

In a different category to the areas above are the **Free Zone** areas, set up in Egypt to encourage local or foreign investors to develop an export market. Profits are exempt from taxes and imports are duty free. Companies and factories operate in these zones as if they were outside the jurisdiction of Egyptian company law.

The General Authority for Investment and Free Zones (**GAFI**) was established by the government to act as a 'one-stop shop' for would be investors, in order to assist them through the bureaucratic maze. GAFI has its offices in the centre of Cairo, significantly alongside the Ministry of Economy.

The Free Zone areas are in Port Said, Alexandria (Amreya), Suez, Ismailia, Damietta and Cairo (Nasr City). At the end of 1998 GAFI reported that of the 518 projects operational in the Free Zones, 231 were in Alexandria, 110 in Cairo, 114 in Port Said and the remainder in the other areas. A further 412 projects were under implementation. America and Britain were the biggest investors in Egypt overall with about two hundred companies each. European companies accounted for over half of the 1,250 foreign companies operations in Egypt at the end of 1998.

Additional development areas are planned. New regional airports and the expansion of existing internal air facilities will, it is hoped by the government, help to distribute the population more evenly over the country and limit the growth of Cairo and Alexandria. The four major developments of Suez, Port Said, Toshka and East Oweinat should be the impetus for this migration. The four desert oases in the south, of which Kharga in the New Valley (Toshka) is the chief, are likely to see population growth and an increase in industry associated with agriculture and local mineral resources. With the

9

major tourist developments under way around Sinai and south from Hurghada, industry and resources will be required to service the expected influx of visitors. Cities will develop in Sinai at Sharm el Sheikh, Nuweiba, Ras Sidr (when a planned airport is complete) and in El Arish – when the peace process in the Middle East is concluded. Mediterranean Sea developments will occur around el Alamein and its new airport, Mersa Matruh (as a gateway to Libya), and to the south, on the Red Sea, Hurghada, Safarga, Quesir and Mersa Allam will develop as Hurghada International Airport is expanded and Mersa Allam Airport is finished. The archaeological resorts of Luxor and Aswan will continue to attract international visitors in increasing numbers and can therefore be expected to expand.

9

10

a break from business

a break from business

From what to do on a spare afternoon
to possible reasons for delaying your
flight back...

A break from business

Although business travellers tend to think themselves too busy to take in a little sightseeing, to turn down the chance to see a little of Egypt is to lose an opportunity to experience a taste of one of the great civilizations of human history. To take an obvious example: absolutely *nobody* can fail to be simply overwhelmed by the sheer scale of the 4000 year-old Pyramids of Giza. If a business visitor to Cairo does nothing else, he or she should just take a taxi out to Giza and wonder.

It is best to avoid summer which, while not unbearably hot like in the Gulf or Saudi Arabia, is unpleasant. Egyptian offices and homes are by no means universally air-conditioned and taxis rarely so.

Summer in the city

Cairenes have become very concerned by the summer humidity and each year comment that it never used to be like this, blaming variously the High Dam at Aswan, global warming, the incessant watering of the streets and the high-rise buildings along the Nile which reduce the airflow through the city.

During the day there are few people about. Traffic is relatively light and shops are empty. During the night however all this changes; the streets become alive. The bridges over the Nile are crowded with people drawn by the cooling Nile breeze. Feluccas and other boats on the water are full of people being entertained with lively music and dance. The riverside bars and cafés are packed. Traffic jams are as bad as any daytime jam in the rest of the year. Shops remain open until late at night or even early morning.

10

A couple of hours spare?

As noted above, the **Pyramids of Giza** are unmissable. Allow two hours (including the taxi ride there and back from the centre of town) for the briefest of visits to the great pyramid of Cheops, his son Chephren and Mycerinus. The restored Sphinx, with its inscrutable smile, will be seen at the funerary temple below the pyramid of Chephren. For those with a little more time on the plateau, a visit to the funerary boat of Cheops could take another half hour, and gluttons for punishment who don't suffer from claustrophobia should allow a further 30 minutes for a visit to the centre of one of the pyramids and to the burial chamber itself. Alternatively, an evening visit to the *son et lumière* show at the pyramids is an interesting and educational experience.

Agricultural monuments on the Nile

Before the dam was built at Aswan there was an annual flood of the Nile Valley which occurred in August and September following the rains in Uganda. This inundation brought with it fertilisers and nutrients and deposited them on the land. The government of that time needed some method of taxing the people and decided that the higher the water reached the more crops would grow and the wealthier farmers would become. Therefore, in order to measure the water level, they built two elaborate structures, one in Upper Egypt and one in Cairo – the Nileometer – which record the level of the river Nile at any time.

A spare hour or two in the centre of Cairo can be well spent at the **Egyptian Museum**, where the star exhibits are undoubtedly the items found in the tomb of the boy king Tutankamoun. The museum has a vast collection of antiquities but the building is old and the displays are badly in need of renovation. A new museum is planned, if and when a site and finance can be arranged. It is said that there are so many artefacts in store at the museum that it will require another archaeological dig to extract them all.

Take a few hours out, preferably during an evening, to walk around **Khan el Khalili**. This is a *suq* or bazaar area within the old walled city of Fatimid Cairo. Apart from the narrow streets and small shops there are some beautiful mosques dating back more than one thousand years, several merchants houses which have been preserved as museums, Islamic libraries, drinking fountains and remains of the city walls and gates. The *suq* has specific areas for particular trades or crafts including the gold *suq*, the street of the tentmakers, and streets specialising in spices, glass, copper and brass,

10

silver, cloth and carpets. Stop at Café Naquib Mafouz (named after the famous Egyptian Nobel Prize winning author) or one of the other many small cafés where tea and coffee are drunk and *shishas* (water pipes) are smoked. Fishawiis, the most famous, has never closed for two hundred years).

For a good view of the city, visit **The Citadel**, which contains the large but undistinguished mosque built by Mohammed Ali, and is where the Mamlukes came to their bloody end. The aqueduct, which was built to supply Nile water to the citadel, can be seen close by. While in the area, two other mosques, those of **Ibn Tulun** and **Sultan Hassan** are very well worth a visit. Next to the Sultan Hassan mosque, the relatively new mosque of **el Rifai**, where the last Shah of Persia is buried, can be visited.

There are plenty of other sights worth a visit. The **Islamic Museum** has a large and interesting collection of art, metalwork, manuscripts and textiles. The **Railway Museum** has early locomotives on view including some sections of the Royal Train. **Coptic Cairo**, is an area with several Christian churches including the so-called Hanging Church, a synagogue and a museum of Coptic art. Close to Coptic Cairo on the southern end of Rhoda Island is the Nileometer.

10

Half Day Trips

The **Pyramids of Saqarra** are about another half an hour's drive beyond the Pyramids of Giza. The oldest pyramid in Egypt, the Step Pyramid, can be seen here together with various temples and underground tombs. The Seraphium, where they buried the sacred bulls, is worth visiting when it is open. From Saqarra, on a clear day, it is possible to see the bent pyramid of Dashur (allow another two hours), the Pyramid of Medun (another half day, see below) and back in the other direction, the Pyramids of Giza.

On the road to Saqarra the **craft village of Wissa Wassef** can be found on the desert side of the road – a small oasis of peace and tranquillity. Wissa Wassef was the originator of the picture rugs seen around Egypt. He believed that all people are born with an artistic ability, which over the years is spoiled by other external influences. There is a gallery of these hand-made rugs, some of which have been exhibited in New York and London.

Day trips

El Alamein – Here can be found Commonwealth and other war grave memorials on the north coast. Also, very moving sites on the old battlefield, largely unchanged since the war.

Monasteries at Wadi Natroun – On the road to Alexandria and about one hour from Cairo are these Coptic walled monasteries in the area where natron, used for preservation and mummification, was excavated.

St. Anthony's Monastery is an interesting Coptic foundation in the desert south of Cairo on the road between Beni Suef and Zafaranaa on the Red Sea. The monastery of St Paul is close by over the mountain, but another hour or more by car.

The **Pyramids of Medun** are two hours south of Cairo on the river. This pyramid is unusual, as it was first a tower; then a pyramid shape was constructed around this central core. Earthquakes subsequently destroyed the pyramid leaving a pile of rubble surrounding the tower. Other pyramids in this complex are of interest, including the double pyramid made from mud bricks.

Ismailia and the Suez Canal. There are many places to see the canal, but Ismailia is probably one of the best places to view the passing ships.

Ain Sukhna. This is one of the nearest Red Sea resorts to Cairo and has a few beach hotels. A good day trip.

It is possible to see **Luxor** and some of its monuments in one day. Very early flights can be arranged from Cairo with a late return the same day. Some travel agents will arrange it all including a guide in Luxor.

Two-Night Excursions

Luxor. A one-day trip, although better than nothing, does not do this place justice. Take two days and see: The Valley of the Kings and its tombs, the Valley of the Queens, the Tombs of the Nobles, Queen Hatshepsut's Temple and Karnak Temple (with a good Son et Lumière). Luxor will make any other monuments in Egypt seem insignificant.

Aswan. Lots to see: the islands in the river, Philae Temple, the High Dam and Lake Nasser, and the new Nubian Museum. Have tea in the Cataract Hotel. Flights from Aswan to the temple at Abu Simbel can be arranged.

10

Sharm el Sheikh, on the Red Sea at the southern tip of Sinai, has hotels catering for all tastes and budgets. Visit Ras Mohammed, the marine nature reserve, for some diving or snorkling over the coral reef.

St Catherine's Monastery, founded by the mother of the Emperor Constantine in the fourth century, is worth a visit. Here it is possible to climb Gebel Mousa or Mount Sinai to see the sun rise over the spectacular mountains. Visit the hippy resort of Dahab, a little way north.

Hurghada is similar to Sharm in style, with many international hotels. To the north El Gouna – a complex of six hotels and golf courses – has been built. Travel south to Safarga, El Quesir and Mersa Allam and visit the tourist resorts of Egypt of the future – before anyone else gets there. Travel overland from here to Luxor and Aswan in two or three hours.

Mersa Matrouh is a Mediterranean resort towards Libya with interesting beaches, a large rock pool known as Queen Cleopatra's Pool and several memorials of World War Two.

Al Arish is a Mediterranean resort town in Sinai. Some remains of the Palestine Railway can be seen including rolling stock and stations.

A Week's Holiday

Nile Cruise. There are cruise boats on the Nile operated by the hotel chains – Sheraton, Oberoi, etc. Boats sail from Luxor to Aswan, or the reverse. The three or four day cruise includes guided visits at Luxor and Aswan and at various sights on the river in between. It is a very relaxing and pleasant way to spend a few days. The best time to go is in the spring or autumn when the weather is more temperate. There are occasional longer cruises available from Cairo.

Lake Nasser Cruise. Recently introduced, these cruises operate on the lake above the Aswan High Dam. The highlight is undoubtedly the visit to Abu Simbel.

The Desert Oases. There are four of these oases: Kharga, Farafra, Baharia and Dakhla. Trips into the desert can be arranged with four wheel drive vehicles and guides.

10

Red Sea Cruising. Diving and fishing cruises, which usually travel south towards Sudan stopping at islands and wrecks on the way, commence at Sharm el Sheikh or Hurghada.

Sinai Trekking. Travel with bedouin guides through Sinai by four wheel drive or four legged camel, camping under the stars.

Shopping in Egypt

Silver and gold. Gold and silver jewellery is available in most hotels. Silver trinkets and dishes are worth buying. There are shops now selling modern jewellery made from silver and local stones; these can be very interesting pieces and reasonably priced.

Copper and brass ornaments are available everywhere. These range from mass-produced, cheap and nasty to interesting and beautifully-worked items.

Perfumes are dubious in quality. However, the perfume bottles are decorative and unusual.

Carpets and rugs are made locally. There are good quality rugs available, but for those travellers who are not too knowledgeable it might be better to take the advice I was once given in a Middle Eastern *suq* when I asked where would be the best place to buy a carpet: 'Go to John Lewis in London'. Picture rugs are typically Egyptian, a nice memento and vary in quality and price. The Wissa Wasef craft village has good but expensive ones.

Spices from the *suq* are probably not fresh. Don't bother.

Antiques are dubious in origin and age. Antiquities of pharaonic or other ancient origin are either fake or illegal to export from the country. There are small shops in Cairo and Alexandria selling recent antiques which have been acquired from local house sales. Furniture, silver and ceramics, imported in the past from Europe are now surfacing but their value seems well known and few bargains are to be had.

Cotton products. Cotton clothing is of excellent quality and reasonably priced, although the better products are made for export and do not reach the local market.

10

Pottery and ceramics. Some may be worth buying and are available in hotels and some small private art galleries.

Papyrus. Pictures painted on papyrus will be thrust at any gullible looking tourist. Some are good, especially those from the famous Dr Raghab, who demonstrates the technique for producing papyrus at his museum.

Entertainment in Egypt

Opera has been popular in Egypt for many centuries, with Verdi writing *Aida* for the Khedive Ismail and the opening of the Suez canal. The opera house in the centre of Cairo burnt down in the 1970s and was replaced in the 1980s by a modern new cultural complex on Gezirah Island, which has art galleries as well as several theatres. Regular concerts and performances are given by local orchestras, choirs and ballet groups. These are good and well worth visiting, not least for the superb setting. Seat prices are very reasonable. Visiting international musicians also perform frequently.

Every October, *Aida* is staged at the Pyramids, in co-operation with an Italian opera company. A spectacular performance, it attracts many visitors from overseas.

Egyptian theatre is alive and well, with several well-attended theatres in the centre of Cairo and Alexandria.

The cinema and film industry in Egypt is huge, the biggest in the Arabic-speaking world – which would explain why most people in the region understand the curious Egyptian Arabic dialect. A major new film production complex is under construction. Cities are dotted with cinemas showing foreign and local releases. Old cinemas are being refurbished and modern multi-screen centres being erected, with a 3D complex just outside Cairo. Drive-in cinema is also being revived.

Each year there is an International Film Festival in Cairo, which from slow local beginnings has evolved into a major event, with many foreign stars visiting Cairo for the week.

There are many private galleries around Cairo and Alexandria which are well worth visiting. Near the Cairo Sheraton hotel in Giza the original home of the Khalil

10

family houses a spectacular private collection of impressionist paintings and ceramics. Adjacent is a new gallery which exhibits visiting collections from around the world. Recently opened in Zamalek, next to the Marriot Hotel, is the Gezirah Art Gallery housing an impressive collection of Islamic ceramics.

10

appendix one

Telephone numbers are changing in Egypt as new technology is introduced. However, it is sometimes difficult to know how and when the numbers might be changed and, indeed, as to what the new numbers might be. The recent advertisement below from the English language press went some way to resolving this.

Make the best use of quality services including ID number,
Call Barring, Follow-me, Alarm, Voice Conference, Non-disturbance, Tone, Hotline Smart network, Integrated network
Egypt Telecom has changed phone numbers of the following telephone exchanges as shown below:
First-Behira-Kafr el-Dawar Telephone Exchange
Numbers have changed from 40.... to 2....
Code number changed from (03) to (045)
Second-Gharbia-10000-line New Santa Telephone Exchange
Numbers starting from 456... to 5462999 are now starting from 547... to 5473... to 5472999 and from 5473... to 5479999
With the compliment of Egypt Telecom

Area codes for the major areas of Egypt are:

Cairo	02
Alexandria	03
Sharm el Sheikh	069

Telephone numbers have recently changed as follows:

Maadi numbers starting with	350 have become	358
	353	519
Garden City	35	79
Mohandaseen (some)	34	74
	36	76
Zamalek (rumoured)	340 to become	735
	341	736
	342	737

Emergencies

Ambulance   123/770123
Police   122/900122/600122
Fire   125/3910115

Credit Card Emergencies

American Express
Nile Tower Building
21 Giza Street
Giza
t: 5703411/5672430/5696111   *f:* 5703146

Cash Cards
3 Abu El Feda Street
Zamalek
t: 3412595/3391855   *f:* 3414010

Diners Club
21 Mohd Mazhar Street
Downtown
t: 3418778   *f:* 3322637

MasterCard/Visa Card
153 Mohamed Farid Street
Bank Misr Tower
t: 35711489/3562966   *f:* 3931415

Business Hotels in Cairo

Baron ★★★★
t: (02) 2915757/2912467   *f:* (02) 2907077

Heliopolis Movenpick
t: (02) 2470077/2919400   *f:* (02) 4180761
e: e-mail@movenpickhel.com.eg

Cairo Marriott ★★★★★
t: (02) 3408888   *f:* (02) 3406667
e: Marriott@link.com.eg
[www.marriotthotels.com]

Pyramids Movenpick
t: (02) 3852555/666   *f:* (02) 3835006

A1

Cairo Sheraton ★★★★★
t: (02) 3369700/800   *f:* (02) 3364601/2
e: Csher@rite.com   [www. sheratonafricamideast.com]

Four Seasons at First
t: (02) 5731212   *f:* (02) 5681616
[www.fourseasons.com]

El-Gezirah Sheraton
t: (02) 3411333/555   *f.* (02) 3405056
e: Gzsher@rite.com

Forte Grand/Meridien Pyramids ★★★★★
t: (02) 3830772   *f:* (02) 3831730
e: c.s@meridien-pyramids.com.eg

Golden Tulip Flamenco ★★★★★
t: (02) 3400815/6   *f:* (02) 3400819
e: Bcflamenco@rite.com

Helnan Shepherd ★★★★★
t: (02) 7953800/900   *f:* (02) 7957284
e: Reshs@helnan.com

Le Meridien Cairo
t: (02) 3621717   *f:* (02) 3621927
e: Mercaic@internetegypt.com

Le Meridien Heliopolis ★★★★★
t: (02) 2905055/2901819   *f:* (02) 4172492
e: Mer-hel1@brainy1.ie-eg.com   [www.meridien.com]

Mena House Oberoi ★★★★★
t: (02) 3833444/222   *f:* (02) 3837777
e: Obmhobc@oberoi.com.eg

Conrad Hilton
t: (02) 5808000   *f:* (02) 5808080
e: Conrad@intouch.com [www.conradhilton.com]

Nile Hilton ★★★★★
t: (02) 5780444/666   *f:* (02) 5780475
e: Nhilton@internetegypt.com   [www.hilton.com]

Hilton Residence at the WTC
t: (02) 5802000   *f:* (02) 5790577

Novotel
t: (02) 2918520   *f:* (02) 2914794

Pyramids Inter-Continental ★★★★
t: (02) 3841444/3838666   *f:* (02) 3839000
e: Pyramids@interconti.com

Pyramisa Hotel Cairo ★★★★★
t: (02) 3367000/8000/9000   *f:* (02) 3605347

President Hotel
t: (02) 3400718/3400652   *f:* (02) 3411752

Ramses Hilton ★★★★★
t: (02) 5758000/5744000   *f:* (02) 5757152
e: Rhinet@intouch.com

Safir ETAP Hotel
t: (02) 3482424/828   *f:* (02) 3608453
e: Safir2@ritsec2.com.eg

Semiramis Inter-Continental
t: (02) 3557171   *f:* (02) 3561320
e: Cairo@interconti.com   [www.interconti.com]

Sheraton Heliopolis Hotel
t: (02) 2677730/40   *f:* (02) 6678170
e: Hsher@rite.com /Sheratonafricamideast.com

Siag Pyramids Hotel ★★★★★
t: (02) 3856022/3005   *f:* (02) 3857413

Sofitel Cairo Maadi Towers ★★★★★
t: (02) 5260601/2   *f:* (02) 5261133

Sofitel Le Sphinx ★★★★★
t: (02) 3837444/555   *f:* (02) 3834930

Sonesta Hotel Cairo ★★★★★
t: (02) 2628111/2617100   *f:* (02) 2635731
e: Sonbc13@brainy1.ie-eg.com

A1

Swissotel Cairo El-Salam ★★★★★
t: (02) 2974000/2976000   *f:* (02) 2976037

Business Hotels in Alexandria

Landmark Hotel
t: (03) 5867850/1   *f:* (03) 5880515

Lord's Inn Center
t: (03) 5462016

Helnan Palestine Hotel ★★★★★
t: (03) 5474033   *f:* (03) 5473378
e: RESHP@helnan.com

Sofitel Alexandria Cecil Hotel
t: (03) 4837173   *f:* (03) 4836401

The Renaissance Hotel
t: (03) 5490935/5483977   *f:* (03) 549760

San Giovanni Hotel
t: (03) 5467774/5   *f:* (03) 5464408

Mercure
t: (03) 5876429   *f:* (03) 5870526

Salamlak
t: (03) 5477999   *f:* (03) 5473585

Sheraton Montazah Hotel
t: (03) 5480550   *f:* (03) 5401331

24 Hour Pharmacies

El-Ezaby
(1) 1 Ahmed Tayseer Street
Heliopolis 11   *t:* (02) 4148467
(2) Syria Street
Mohandiseen   *t:* 3041647

El-Rahma Drug Store
35 Rd.276
New Maadi
Maadi   *t:* 5191568

Essam
101 Rd.9
Maadi
t: 3584126

Isaaf
Ramses Street
Corner of 26th of July Street
t: 5743369

Zamalek
3 Shagaret El Dorr Street
Zamalek
t: 3416424

Hospitals

Anglo-American Hospital
Next to Cairo Tower
Zamalek
t: 3406162

Arab Contractors Medical Centre
El Gabal El Akhdar
Nasr Road
t: 2830000   *f:* 2821624

Cairo Medical Centre
4 Abu Ebeida El Bakry Street
Roxy Square
Heliopolis
t: 2581003   *f:* 4521074

Cleopatra Hospital
39 Cleopatra Street
Salah El Din Square
t: 2914590   *f:* 4178206

El-Salam Hospital (BUPA)
3 Syria Street
Mohandiseen
t: 30290915   *f:* 3030140

El-Salam International Hospital (BUPA)
Corniche El Nil, Maadi
t: 5240250   *f:* 5240066

A1

Heliopolis Hospital
Hegaz Street , Heliopolis
t: (02) 2444991/2371000   *f:* (02) 2445726

Kasr El-Aini Hospital
Roda island, North End
t: 3643805   *f:* 3643884

Nile Badrawi Hospital
Corniche El Nil, Maadi
t: 3638688   *f:* 3629910/3638684

Airlines
Air Canada
c/o Imperial Travel
26 Mahmoud Bassiouni Street, Downtown
t: 5758939/402/939   *f:* 5749129
[www.aircanada.ca]

Air France
2 Talaat Harb Square, Downtown
t: 5758899   *f:* 771744
[www.airfrance.com]

Air Malta
c/o Emeco Travel
2 Talaat Harb Street, Downtown
t: 5749360   *f:* 5744212
[www.airmalta.com]

Alitalia
(1) Nile Hilton Hotel, Tahrir Square
t: 5785823-5
(2) Cairo Airport
t: 4188168   *f:* 779907
[www.alitalia.it/eng]

American Airlines
20 El Gihad Street, Mohandiseen
t: 3455707/3470033

Austrian Airlines
4 Mamar Behler, Off Kasr El Nil, Downtown
t: 3921522   *f:* 3916080
[www.aua.com]

British Airways
(1) 1 Abd El Salam Arif Street, Tahrir Square
t: 5780742/5747674
(2) Maadi
t: 3582264-5   *f:* 5780739
(3) Cairo Airport
t: (02) 4175681-3
[www.british-airways.com]

Cathay Pacific
20 El Gihad Street, Mohandiseen
t: 3029627   *f:* 3030593
[www.cathaypacific.com]

Continental Airlines
c/o Imperial Travel
26 Mahmoud Bassiouni Street, Downtown
t: 5758939   *f:* 5749129
[www.continental.com]

Cyprus Air
c/o Bon Voyage 16 Adli Street, Downtown
t: 3907669/3912345   *f:* 3911104
[www.cyprusair.com]

A1

Delta Airlines
c/o Five Continents
Jeddah Tower
17 Ismail Mohammed Street
Zamalek
t: 3420861/3401948   *f:* 3419626
[www.delta-air.com]

EgyptAir
(1) 9 Taalaat Harb Street, Downtown
t: 3932836   *f:* 3901557
(2) Nile Hilton Hotel   *t:* 765200
(3) Movenpick Hotel   *t:* 2455793
(4) Cairo Sheraton   *t:* 3488630
(5) 26th July St, Mohandiseen   *t:* 3472027
(6) 22 Ibrahim El Lakani St. Heliopolis *t:* 2904528
(7) Cairo Airport   *t:* 2441460   *f:* 2459316
[www.egyptair.com]

El Al Israel Airlines
5 El Makrizi Street, Zamalek
t: 3411795/620   *f:* 3411620
[www.elal.co.il]

Emirates Airlines
18 Ahmed Abdul Aziz St, Mohandaseen
t: 3361555   *f:* 7484138
[www.ekgroup.com]

Gulf Air
(1) 64 Gameat El Dowal
El Arabia Street, Mohandiseen
t: 3484116/ 3487781/3495018
(2) 21 Mahmoud Bassiouni Street, Downtown
t: 5758391/3490955   *f:* 5749129
[www.gulfairco.com]

Iberia Airlines
(1) 15 Tahrir Square
t: 5789955/760656
(2) Cairo Airport
t: 4177297   *f:* 2905190
[www.iberia.com]

Japan Airlines (JAL)
Nile Hilton Hotel, Tahrir Square
t: 5747233   *f:* 5747232
[www.jal.co.jp/english/index_e.html]

KLM
(1) 11 Kasr El Nil Street, Downtown
t: 5747004/5748004
(2) Cairo Airport
t: 4182386   *f:* 5747330
[www.klm.com]

Kuwait Airways
(1) 4 Taalaat Harb Street, Downtown
t: 5742135
(2)24 Ibrahim El Lakani Street, Heliopolis *t:* 660006
(3) Mohandiseen   *t:* 3440471
(4) Cairo Airport   *t:* 2919591 *f:*5742747
[www.Travelfirst.com/sub/kuwaitair.html]

Lufthansa
(1) 6 El Sheikh El Marsafi Street, Zamalek
t: 3398339
(2) Cairo Airport
t: 4176419   *f:* 3407981
[www.lufthansa.com]

Malaysian Airlines
10 Commercial Center
Nile Hilton
t: 5799714/578155   *f:* 5799713
[www.malaysiaairlines.com.my]

Middle East Airlines
12, Kasr El Nil Street, Downtown
t: 5750888   *f:* 5742157
[www.mea.com/lb]

Olympic Airways
23 Kasr El Nil Street, Downtown
t: 3931277   *f:* 3910574
[www.olympicair.com]

Oman Air
C/o Travco, 44 Mohammed Mazhar St.
t: 3422940   *f:* 3422462

Pakistan International Airlines
(1) 22 Kasr El Nil Street, Downtown
t: 3924055/3422940   *f:* 674154
(2) Cairo Airport
t: 3931604
[www.piac.com/index.htm]

Royal Jordanian
(1) 6 Kasr El Nil Street, Downtown
t: 5750875
(2) Cairo Airport
t: 668903   *f:* 3462446
[www.rja.com.jo]

Scandinavian Airlines System
2 Champollion Street, Downtown
t: 5741089/5753627   *f:* 5750574
[www.sas.sc]

A1

Saudi Arabian Airlines
(1) 5 Kasr El Nil Street, Downtown
t: 5747388
(2) Cairo Airport
t: 2907036　　　　　　　*f:* 766271
[www.saudiairlines.com]

Singapore Airlines
(1) Nile Hilton Hotel, Tahrir Square
t: 2915242
(2) Cairo Airport
t: 5750276　　　　　　　*f:* 767387
[www.singaporeair.com]

Swissair
(1) 4 Behler Passage
Kasr El Nil
Reservations　　*t:* 3921522　Information　*t:* 3937955
(2) Cairo Airport　*t:* 2910283　*f:* 3916080
[www.swissair.ch]

Syrian Arab Airlines
(1) 25 Taalaat Harb Street, Downtown
t: 3928284
(2) Cairo Airport
t: 3928284 Ext. 4890　　　　*f:* 3910805

TWA
(1) 1 Kasr El Nil Street, Downtown
t: 5749904
(2) Cairo Airport
t: 2441050　　　　　　　*f:* 5749909
[www.twa.com]

United Airlines
c/o Lufthansa, 6 El Sheikh El Marsafi Street
Zamalek
t: 3398566　　　　　　　*f:* 3407599
[www.ual.com]

Airports
Alexandria
(1) Nozha Airport
t: (03) 4202021
(2) Borg al Arab
t: (03) 4591485/6/7

A1

Aswan
t: (097) 480320/33

Cairo International Airport
t: 2914255/66/77
Arrival Hall 1. *t:* 2441460   Arrival Hall 2   *t:* 2459332

Hurghada
t: (065) 442831/443976

Luxor
t: (095) 374655

Sharm El-Sheikh
t: (069) 600314/600664

Automobile/Limousine Rentals

Alex Limousine
33 El Tawfik Street, Nasr City
t: 4017251/350

Alkan Car Hire
2 Messaha Square, Dokki
t: 3490140   *f:* 3499253/3609932

Avis
16a Maamal El Sukkar Street, Garden City
t: 3547400/ 3548698

Bita Car Rental
(1) 73 El Nozha Street, Manshiet El Bakry
t: 4542620
(2) 23 Dr. Ahmed Zaki Street El Nozha, El Gedida
t: 2991527   *f:* 2991799/601082

Budget Rent-A-Car
(1) 5 El Makrizi Street, Zamalek
t: 3400070/3409474
(2) Marriott Hotel
t: 3408888
(3) Cairo Airport
t: 2914288   *f:* 3413790

A1

A1

Egytrav
Nile Hilton Hotel, Tahrir Square
t: 5755029   *f:* 778861

Elite Rent-A-Car
2 Tahran Street, Dokki Giza
t: 3609976   *f:* 3481984

Europcar/InterRent Egypt
Max Building, 27 Lebanon Street Mohandiseen
t: 3474712/3451022   *f:* 3036123

Fast Car Rental
7 Yanboa St. Dokki
t: 3613743   *f:* 3483937

Hertz Rent-A-Car
195, 26th July Street, Agouza
t: 3034241   *f:* 3446627

Iveco
22 Mahmoud Bassiouni Street
t: 759061/747006

Kadry Motor Co.
29 Amin El Rifaii Street, Messaha Square,
t: 347413   *f:* 3036123

Limo One Rent-A-Car
159, 26th of July Street, Zamalek
t: 3405920   *f:* 3404817

Limousine Misr
Misr Travel Tower, 13th floor, Abassiya Square
t: 2856721   *f:* 2856124

Mohammed Hafez Co.
4a Harroun Street, Dokki
t: 3600542/3486652   *f:* 3481105

Payless Car Rental
31 Mohammed Farid St. Heliopolis
t: 2455555   2472470

Rawas Car and Limousine Rental
(1)4 Tahran Square, Off Mossadak Street, Dokki
t: 3499831/3350477
(2) Gezirah Sheraton Hotel
t: 3411333 Ext. 8341
(3) Ramses Hilton Hotel
t: 777444   *f:* 3499831

Sahara Rent-A-Car
14 Tiba Street, Mohandiseen
t: 3488958/3491472

Shahd Limousine
34 El-Falah St. Mohandiseen
t: 3454516   *f:* 3454563

Smart Limo
151 Corniche El Nil
t: 5243006   *f:* 5243009

Banks

American Express Bank
4 Syria Street, Mohandiseen
t: 3605258   *f:*3608227

Arab Bank PLC
50 Gezirat El Arab Street, Mohandiseen
t: 3029069   *f:* 3029068

Banque Du Caire
30 Roushdi Street, Abdeen, PO Box 1495
t: 3908850   *f:* 3903405

Banque Du Caire et De Paris
3 Latin America Street, Garden City
t: 7948323   *f:* 7940619

Banque Paribas
6a Ghandi Street, Garden City
t: 7940391   *f:* 7955082

Barclays International
12 Midan El Sheikh Youssef, Garden City
t: 7949415   *f:*7952746

A1

Central Bank of Egypt
31 Kasr El Nil Street
t: 3926211 *f:* 3926361

Chase Manhattan Bank
3 Ahmed Nessim St. Giza
t: 3610393 *f:* 3610498

Citibank
(1)4 Ahmed Pasha Street, Garden City
t: 7951873 *f:* 7957743
(2) Zamalek Branch (24 hours)
t: 3405238 *f:* 3404962

Credit Lyonnais
3 Yemen Street, Giza
t: 3379622 *f:* 3606458

Delta International Bank
1113 Corniche El Nil
t: 5753492 *f:* 5740928

Deutsche Bank
23 Kasr El Nil Street
t: 3922341 *f:* 3922341

Egyptian American Bank
4/6 Hassan Sabri Street, Zamalek
t: 3400063 *f:* 3409430

Egyptian British Bank
3 Abu El Feda Street, Zamalek
t: 3409186 *f:* 3414010

Misr America International Bank
12 Nadi El Seid Street, Dokki
t: 3616615 *f:* 3616610

National Bank of Egypt
24 Sherif Street, Downtown
t: 3924022 *f:* 3936481

Société Génerale
3 Abu El Feda Street, Zamalek
t: 3411627 *f:* 3411636

A1

Chambers of Commerce

American Chamber of Commerce
33, Soliman Abaza Street
t: 3381050   *f:* 3380850
e: Acce@ritsec1.com.eg

British Egyptian Business Association (BEBA)
124 Nile St. Agouza
t: 3491401   *f:* 3491421
e: Egyptuk@beba.com

Cairo Chamber of Commerce
4 El Falaki Square. Downtown
t: 3558261   *f:* 3563603

Club D'Affaires Franco-Egyptian
5 Shagaret El Dorr Street, 2nd Floor, Apt 11, Zamalek
t: 3322666   *f:* 3404959

Egyptian American Businessmen's Association
Nile Tower, 21 Giza Street, Giza
t: 737258/736030

Egyptian Businessmen's Association
Nile Tower, 16th floor 21 Giza St. Giza
*t:*5723855   *f:* 5737258

Federation of Egyptian Chambers of Commerce
4 Sherif Street,
t: 3958367   *f:* 3958371

Federation of Egyptian Industries
28a Corniche El Nil
t: 5796590   *f:* 5796593

German-Arab Chamber of Commerce in Egypt
3 Abu El Feda St., Zamalek
t: 3413664   *f:* 3413663
e: Fit@gerarcham.com

Courier Services

ARAMEX - International Courier
14 Yehia Ibrahim St. Zamalek 4 Tael El Ahwal Street,
Heliopolis
t: 3322225 2456369   *f:* 3322258

A1

DHL
(1) Head Office - 16 Lebanon Street, Mohandiseen
t: 3029801   *f:* 3029810
(2) 20 Gamal El Din Abu El Mahassin St., Garden City
t: 7957118
(3) 34 Abd El Khalek Tharwat St., Downtown
t: 3938988
(4) Maadi
t: 3758900

Express Mail Service (EMS)
Ataba Square
t: 3905874

IML Air Couriers
2 Mustafa Kamel Street, Maadi
t: 3581160   *f:* 3581240

Middle East Couriers
1 Mahmoud Hafez Street, Safir Square,
PO Box 2471, Heliopolis
t: 2459281   *f:* 2404909

SOS Sky International
29 Hamadan St. Giza
t: 5723077

TNT Skypack
33 Dokki St. Dokki
t: 3418527   *f:* 3486422

UPS
7 Hussein Zohdy St Golf Area, Nasr City
t: 4154885   *f:* 4141457

World Courier Egypt
17 Kasr El Nil St. Downtown
t: 777678

Embassies
Australia
World Trade Centre, 11th Flr, Boulac
t: 5750444/5780650   *f:* 5781638

Austria
Wissa Wassef/El Nil Street, Giza
t: 5702974   *f:* 5702979

Bahrain
15 Brasil Street Zamalek
t: 3416605   *f:* 3416609

Belgium
20 Kamel El Shinnawi Street, Garden City
t: 7947494   *f:* 7943147

Canada
Arab African Bank Bld, 5 Soraya El Kobra Sq,
Garden City
t: 7943110   *f:* 7963548

China
22 Baghat Aly Street, Zamalek
t: 3416561/3417423   *f:* 3412094

Commission of Europe
6 Ibn Zanki Street, Zamalek
t: 3419393/3408388   *f:* 3400385

Cuba
14 El Medina El Munawarra Street, Dokki
t: 3371649   *f:* 3350390

Cyprus
23a Ismail Mohd Street, Zamalek
t: 3411288   *f:* 3415299

Denmark
12 Hassan Sabri Street, Zamalek
t: 3407411/3402502   *f:* 3411780

Finland
3 Abu El Feda Street, Zamalek
t: 3411487   *f:* 3405170

France
29 Murad Street, Giza
t: 5703919   *f:* 5710276

A1

Germany
8b Hassan Sabri, Zamalek
t: 3410015/3399600   *f:* 3410530

Ghana
1 26th July Street, Lebanon Square
t: 3032294/3444000   *f:* 3032292

Great Britain
7 Ahmed Raghab Street, Garden City
t: 7940852   *f:* 7940859

Greece
18 Aisha El Taimouria Street, Garden City
t: 7955915   *f:* 7963903

Hungary
29 Mohd El Mahzar Street, Zamalek
t: 3408634   *f:* 3408648

India
5 Aziz Abaza Street, Zamalek
t: 3413051   *f:* 3414038

Iran
12 Amin El Rifai Street, Dokki
t: 3486492   *f:* 3496821

Iraq
9 Mohd El Mahzar Street, Zamalek
t: 3408087   *f:* 3415075

Ireland
3 Abou El Feda Street, Zamalek
t: 3408547   *f:* 3412863

Israel
6 Ibn Malik Street, Giza
t: 3610545   *f:* 3610414

Italy
15 Abd El Rahman Fahmy Street, Garden City
t: 7940658/7943195   *f:* 7940657

A1

Japan
Cairo Centre Bldg, Kasr El Aini, Garden City
t: 7953963   *f:* 7963540

Jordan
6 El geheini Street, Dokki
t: 3485566/3486169   *f:* 3601027

Kenya
7 El Mohandis Galal Street, Mohandaseen
t: 3453628   *f:* 3443400

Kuwait
12 Nabil El Waqad Street, Dokki
t: 3602661   *f:* 3602657

Lebanon
22 El Mansour Mohd Street, Zamalek
t: 3322823   *f:* 3322818

Libya
7 El Saleh Ayoub Street, Zamalek
t: 3401269/3405439   *f:* 3400072

A1

Malaysia
29 Taha Hussein Street, Zamalek
t: 3410863   *f:* 3411049/3416192

Malta
25 Road 12, Maadi
t: 3754451/7900655   *f:* 3754452

Mexico
17 Port Said Street, Maadi
t: 3580258   *f:* 3581887

Morocco
10 Salah El Din Street, Zamalek
t: 3409849   *f:* 3411937

Netherlands
18 Hassan Sabri Street, Zamalek
t: 3401936   *f:* 3415249

Nigeria
13 El Gabalaya Street, Zamalek
t: 3417894   *f:* 3407359

North Korea
6 El Saleh Ayoub Street, Zamalek
t: 3419532   *f:* 3418519

Norway
8 El Gezirah Street, Zamalek
t: 3413955   *f:* 3420709

Oman
52 El Hegaz Street, Mohandaseen
t: 3036011   *f:* 3036464

Pakistan
8 El Seluli Street, Dokki
t: 3487677   *f:* 3480310

Philippines
14 Mohamed Salah Street, Dokki
t: 3480396   *f:* 3480393

Poland
5 Aziz Osman Street, Zamalek
t: 3405416/3409583   *f:* 3405427

Portugal
57 Giza Street, Giza
t: 3363950   *f:* 3363952

Qatar
10 El Therma Street, Dokki
t: 3604693   *f:* 3603618

Romania
6 El Kamal Mohamed Street, Zamalek
t: 3410107   *f:* 3410851/3930102

Russia
95 Giza Street Giza
t: 3489353/3489744   *f:* 3609074

A1

Saudi Arabia
2 Ahmed nessim Street, Giza
t: 3490797/3490775   *f:* 3494590/3493495

Singapore
40 Babel Street, Dokki
t: 3490468   *f:* 3481682

South Africa
Nile Tower, 21 Giza Street, Giza
t: 5717234   *f:* 5717241

South Korea
3, Boulos Hanna Street, Dokki
t: 3611234   *f:* 3611238

Spain
41, Ismail Mohd Street, Zamalek
t: 3406437/3405813   *f:* 3402132

Sudan
3 El Ibrahim Street, Garden City
t: 7945043   *f:* 7942693

A1

Sweden
13 Mohd Mazhar Street, Zamalek
t: 3411484   *f:* 3404357

Switzerland
10 Abd El Khalek Tharwat Street, Downtown
t: 765719/5758284   *f:* 5745236

Syria
18 Abd El Rehim Sabri Street, Dokki
t: 3358320   *f:* 3358232

Tunisia
26 El Gezirah Street, Zamalek
t: 3418962   *f:* 3412479

Turkey
25 El Falaki Street, Bab El Louk
t: 3563318   *f:* 3558110

United Arab Emirates
4 Ibn Sina Street, Giza
t: 3609722   *f:* 5700844

United States of America
8 Kamal El Din Street, Garden City
t: 7957371   *f:* 7973200

Yemen
28 Amin El Rifai Street, Dokki
t: 3614224   *f:* 3604815

Yugoslavia
33 El Mansour Mohd Street, Zamalek
t: 3404061   *f:* 3403913

Zambia
25 Abd El Moneim Riyadh Street
t: 3610821   *f:* 3610833

appendix two

appendix two

Arabic – The Language of Egypt

The Arabic language exists at its purest in the written word of the Quran, and in spite of the fact that this was first committed to paper more than 1,300 years ago, is still universally understood across the Middle East. The spoken word has evolved considerably from this common basis, however, with different dialects spoken in each country. The Arabic spoken in Egypt is curiously distinct, and, following from Cairo's success in establishing itself as the centre of film production across the region back in the 1950s, Egyptian Arabic is now universally understood.

Most expatriates will learn some Arabic while they are living in Egypt. Some will become proficient, others will merely learn to get by – I fall into this latter group. Most Egyptians can at the very least get by in English and, indeed, it is humbling to sit in a restaurant in Cairo or Sharm El Sheikh and to discuss the menu in English with the waiter, to find that he will pass to the next table and carry on a similar conversation in French or Italian with easy fluency.

To help gain a good understanding of spoken Arabic, it is a good idea to learn the written text at the same time - it is then possible to read road or shop signs, newspapers etc. Practising your spoken Arabic is often made difficult by the fact that any Egyptian in the company of an English speaker will want to practise his English. I invariably end up in taxis (good captive audiences if you persevere) speaking Arabic, while the driver speaks English.

However, a few words of Arabic are worth having. For one thing it enables the business executive to give the impression of fluency and this discourages Arabic asides during a meeting. It is also a basic courtesy to be able to say 'Good Morning', 'How are you', etc. and comforting to be able to give directions to drivers - 'Turn left', 'After half an hour', etc.

The spoken Arabic of Cairo is difficult to transliterate. There are, moreover, two extra sounds used in the language that are difficult for a western tongue to handle. One sounds similar to a glottal stop (the *'ein*) and the other sound is similar to someone clearing their throat (the *kha*). To master these sounds requires a lot of

A2

practice and patience from the listener, but without these sounds some words become completely different and this can lead to considerable confusion and possibly embarrassment. Another difficulty is the lack of the letter 'p' in their language, causing confusion when they translate back into English!

Basic Phrases
Greetings

Good-morning	*Sabaa al kheir*
Reply	*Sabaa al nour* (have a bright one)
or	*Sabaa al fool* (let it smell like jasmine)
or	*Sabaa al ishtar* (let it be rich and creamy - guaranteed to raise a laugh)
Good-afternoon	*Maas al kheir*
Reply	*Maas al nour*
Hello	*Maahaba* (rarely used in Egypt)
Goodbye	*Maa salaama*
Good-night	*Tiss baa alla kheir*

(when leaving at night or going to bed)

Reply	*Wa inta min ahl al kheir*
How are you?	*Izzayak (m), Izzayik (f)*
Fine, thank you	*Quais, al humdulillah* (Good, thanks be to God)
What's your name?	*ismak eh? (m)* *ismik eh? (f)*

(as frequently used by small boys in the street)

My name is....	*ismi ....*

Common expressions

Thank you	*shukran*
I do not understand	*mish* (not) *faahim*
Do you speak English?	*bi kalam Inglizi?*
What ....?	*eh.....?*
What is this?	*eh, da?*

A2

Where ....?	*fane...?*
Where is the bathroom?	*fane hammam?*
How much (money)?	*bikaam?*
How many?	*kaam?*
Why?	*lay?*
Here	*hinna*
There	*hinnaak*
God willing	*inshallah*

(frequently used in many circumstances)

Yes	*aywah, naam*
No	*la*
(or, to emphasise,	*la'a*)
And	*wa, u*
Never mind	*maa leesh*
I mean...	*yaani...*

(trendy expression, tends to irritate if used too often)

Again	*kamaan*
Also	*baardu*
OK	*maashi*
No problem	*mafi mushkala*

(all-purpose phrase, e.g. when you have reversed into someone's car.

It is possible	*mumkin*
It is not possible	*mish mumkin*
Finish, stop	*khalaas*

(as in 'You have reversed into my car!')

Excellent	*miyya miyya* (100%)
Not bad	*nuss u nuss* (half and half)
Only, stop, enough	*bass*

(as in 'Stop reversing into my car!')

Congratulations	*maabruk*
Me	*anna*
Foreigner	*khawaaga*
Broken	*maksoor*
Up	*fouq*
Down	*taht*
After	*baad*
With	*maa*
With sugar	*maa sookar*
Without	*bedoon*
Without milk	*bedoon haleeb*
Tea	*chai*
Coffee	*ghower*
Electricity	*carabaa*
No electricity	*maafish carabaa*

A2

A2

Locations

Airport	*mataar*
Bridge	*kubri*
Embassy	*safaraa*
British Embassy	*safaraa Britania*
Ambassador	*safeer*
Home, house	*bayt*
My home	*bayti*
Your home	*bayti (m) baytak (f)*
My home is your home	*bayti baytak*
Hospital	*mustashfa*
Hotel	*funduq*
Sheraton Hotel	*funduq Sheraton*
Bazaar, shops	*sooq*
Office	*maktab*
My office	*maktabi*
School	*madrassa*
Square	*medan*
Mustafa Kamel Sq	*medan Mustafa Kamel*
Street	*shaarih*
Egypt	*Masr*

(although normally written as Misr on signs, etc)

Directions

Ahead, straight on	*alla tool*
Right	*yameen*
Left	*ashmaal*
After	*baad*
Near	*gamb*
Stop here	*hinna quais* (here good)

Money

Pound	*guinea*
Egyptian pound	*guinea mussry*
Piastres	*irsh* or *piastres*
.... and a half	.... *u nuss*
.... and a quarter	.... *u ruber*
.... less a quarter	.... *illa ruber*

(3.75LE = 4 less a quarter or *arbaa guinea illa ruber*)

Change	*faaka*
No change	*maafish faaka*
How much?	*bikam*
Too much	*kitir*

Numbers

one	*wahad*
two	*itnayn*
three	*tellata*
four	*arbaa*
five	*khamsa*
six	*setta*
seven	*sabaa*
eight	*temanya*
nine	*tissa*
ten	*ashera*
eleven	*ihdasha*
twelve	*itnasha*
thirteen	*tellatasha*
fourteen	*arbaatasha*
fifteen	*khamastasha*
sixteen	*settasha*
seventeen	*sabaatasha*
eighteen	*temantasha*
nineteen	*tissatasha*
twenty	*isherene*
thirty	*tellatene*
forty	*arbaarene*
fifty	*khamsene*
sixty	*settene*
seventy	*sabaayene*
eighty	*temanene*
ninety	*tissayene*
one hundred	*miyye*
one thousand	*alf*
two thousand	*alfayn*

A2

Time

Today	*nehaada*

('I'll do it immediately' becomes *harda* or 'some time today')

Later	*badayn*
Now	*delwahty*
Tomorrow	*bukra*
After tomorrow	*baad bukra*
Yesterday	*imbarrah*
Before yesterday	*awahl imbarrah*
Morning	*subh*
Afternoon	*baad i dour*
Night	*bilayl*

Sunday	*il had* (*wahad* - one)
Monday	*il itenaen* (*itnaen* - two)
Tuesday	*ittellata* (*tellata* - three)
Wednesday	*il arbaa* (*arbaa* - four)
Thursday	*il khamees* (*khamsa* - five)
Friday	*il gomma*
Saturday	*issabt*
One o'clock	*issaah wahada*
Two o'clock	*issaah itnaen*
Half past three	*issaah tellata u nuss*

A2

appendix three
commercial support
for US companies

appendix three

Directory of Export Assistance Centers

Cities in capital letters are centres which combine the export promotion and trade finance service of the Department of Commerce, the Export-Import Bank, the Small Business Administration and the Agency of International Development.

ALABAMA
Birmingham, Alabama - George Norton, Director
950 22nd Street North, Room 707, ZIP 35203
t: : (205) 731-1331   *f:* (205) 731-0076

ALASKA
Anchorage, Alaska - Charles Becker, Director
550 West 7th Ave., Suite 1770, ZIP: 99501
t: (907) 271-6237   *f:* (907) 271-6242

ARIZONA
Phoenix, Arizona - Frank Woods, Director
2901 N. Central Ave., Suite 970, ZIP 85012
t: (602) 640-2513   *f:* (602) 640-2518

CALIFORNIA - LONG BEACH
Joseph F Sachs, Director
Mary Delmege, CS Director
One World Trade Center, Ste. 1670, ZIP: 90831
t: (562) 980-4550   *f:* (562) 980-4561

CALIFORNIA - SAN JOSE
101 Park Center Plaza, Ste. 1001, ZIP: 95113
t: (408) 271-7300   *f:* (408) 271-7307

COLORADO - DENVER
Nancy Charles-Parker, Director
1625 Broadway, Suite 680, ZIP: 80202
t: (303) 844-6623   *f:* (303) 844-5651

A3

CONNECTICUT

Middletown, Connecticut - Carl Jacobsen, Director
213 Court Street, Suite 903 ZIP: 06457-3346
t: (860) 638-6950   *f:* (860) 638-6970

DELAWARE

Served by the Philadelphia, Pennsylvania U.S. Export
AssistanceCenter

FLORIDA - MIAMI

John McCartney, Director
P.O. Box 590570, ZIP: 33159
5600 Northwest 36th St., Ste. 617, ZIP: 33166
t: (305) 526-7425   *f:* (305) 526-7434

GEORGIA - ATLANTA

Samuel Troy, Director
285 Peachtree Center Avenue, NE, Suite 200
ZIP: 30303-1229
t: (404) 657-1900   *f:* (404) 657-1970

HAWAII

Honolulu, Hawaii - Greg Wong, Manager
1001 Bishop St.; Pacific Tower; Suite 1140
ZIP: 96813
t: (808) 522-8040   *f:* (808) 522-8045

IDAHO

Boise, Idaho - James Hellwig, Manager
700 West State Street, 2nd Floor, ZIP: 83720
t: (208) 334-3857   *f:* (208) 334-2783

ILLINOIS - CHICAGO

Mary Joyce, Director
55 West Monroe Street, Suite 2440, ZIP: 60603
t: (312) 353-8045   *f:* (312) 353-8120

A3

INDIANA

Indianapolis, Indiana - Dan Swart, Manager
11405 N. Pennsylvania Street, Suite 106
Carmel, IN, ZIP: 46032
t: (317) 582-2300   **f:** (317) 582-2301

IOWA

Des Moines, Iowa - Allen Patch, Director
601 Locust Street, Suite 100, ZIP: 50309-3739
t: (515) 288-8614   **f:** (515) 288-1437

KANSAS

Wichita, Kansas - George D. Lavid, Manager
209 East William, Suite 300, ZIP: 67202-4001
t: (316) 269-6160   **f:** (316) 269-6111

KENTUCKY

Louisville, Kentucky - John Autin, Director
601 W. Broadway, Room 634B , ZIP: 40202
t: (502) 582-5066   **f:** (502) 582-6573

A3

LOUISIANA - DELTA

Patricia Holt, Acting Director
365 Canal Street, Suite 1170
New Orleans ZIP: 70130
t: (504) 589-6546   **f:** (504) 589-2337

MAINE

Portland, Maine - Jeffrey Porter, Manager
c/o Maine International Trade Center
511 Congress Street, ZIP: 04101
t: (207) 541-7400   **f:** (207) 541-7420

MARYLAND - BALITMORE

Michael Keaveny, Director
World Trade Center, Suite 2432
401 East Pratt Street, ZIP: 21202
t: (410) 962-4539   **f:** (410) 962-4529

MASSACHUSETTS - BOSTON
Frank J. O'Connor, Director
164 Northern Avenue
World Trade Center, Suite 307, ZIP: 02210
t: (617) 424-5990   **f:** (617) 424-5992

MICHIGAN - DETROIT
Neil Hesse, Director
211 W. Fort Street, Suite 2220, ZIP: 48226
t: (313) 226-3650   **f:** (313) 226-3657

MINNESOTA - MINNEAPOLIS
Ronald E. Kramer, Director
45 South 7th St., Suite 2240, ZIP: 55402
t: (612) 348-1638   **f:** (612) 348-1650

MISSISSIPPI
Mississippi - Harrison Ford, Manager
704 East Main St., Raymond, MS, ZIP: 39154
t: (601) 857-0128   **f:** (601) 857-0026

MISSOURI - ST LOUIS
Randall J. LaBounty, Director
8182 Maryland Avenue, Suite 303, ZIP: 63105
t: (314) 425-3302   **f:** (314) 425-3381

MONTANA
Missoula, Montana - Mark Peters, Manager
c/o Montana World Trade Center
Gallagher Business Bldg., Suite 257, ZIP: 59812
t: (406) 243-2098   **f:** (406) 243-5259

NEBRASKA
Omaha, Nebraska - Meredith Bond, Manager
11135 "O" Street, ZIP: 68137
t: (402) 221-3664   **f:** (402) 221-3668

A3

NEVADA
Reno, Nevada - Jere Dabbs, Manager
1755 East Plumb Lane, Suite 152, ZIP: 89502
t: (702) 784-5203   **f:** (702) 784-5343

NEW HAMPSHIRE
Portsmouth, New Hampshire - Susan Berry, Manager
17 New Hampshire Avenue, ZIP: 03801-2838
t: (603) 334-6074   **f:** (603) 334-6110

NEW JERSEY
Trenton, New Jersey - Rod Stuart, Director
3131 Princeton Pike, Bldg. #4, Suite 105, ZIP: 08648
t: (609) 989-2100   **f:** (609) 989-2395

NEW MEXICO
New Mexico - Sandra Necessary, Manager
c/o New Mexico Dept. of Economic Development
P.O. Box 20003, Santa Fe, ZIP: 87504-5003
FEDEX:1100 St. Francis Drive, ZIP: 87503
t: (505) 827-0350   **f:** (505) 827-0263

NEW YORK - NEW YORK
John Lavelle, Acting Director
6 World Trade Center, Rm. 635, ZIP: 10048
t: (212) 466-5222   **f:** (212) 264-1356

NORTH CAROLINA - CAROLINAS
Roger Fortner, Director
521 East Morehead Street, Suite 435, Charlotte, ZIP:
28202
t: (704) 333-4886   **f:** (704) 332-2681

NORTH DAKOTA
Served by the Minneapolis, Minnesota Export
Assistance Center

A3

OHIIO - CLEVELAND
Michael Miller, Director
600 Superior Avenue, East, Suite 700
ZIP: 44114
t: (216) 522-4750   *f:* (216) 522-2235

OKLAHOMA
Oklahoma City, Oklahoma - Ronald L. Wilson, Director
301 Northwest 63rd Street, Suite 330, ZIP: 73116
t: (405) 608-5302   *f:* (405) 608-4211

OREGON - PORTLAND
Scott Goddin, Director
One World Trade Center, Suite 242
121 SW Salmon Street, ZIP: 97204
t: (503) 326-3001   *f:* (503) 326-6351

PENNSYLVANIA - PHILADELPHIA
Rod Stuart, Acting Director
615 Chestnut Street, Ste. 1501, ZIP: 19106
t: (215) 597-6101   *f:* (215) 597-6123

PUERTO RICO
San Juan, Puerto Rico (Hato Rey) - Vacant, Manager
525 F.D. Roosevelt Avenue, Suite 905
ZIP: 00918
t: (787) 766-5555   *f:* (787) 766-5692

RHODE ISLAND
Providence, Rhode Island - Vacant, Manager
One West Exchange Street, ZIP: 02903
t: (401) 528-5104, *f:* (401) 528-5067

SOUTH CAROLINA
Columbia, South Carolina - Ann Watts, Director
1835 Assembly Street, Suite 172, ZIP: 29201
t: (803) 765-5345   *f:* (803) 253-3614

A3

SOUTH DAKOTA
Siouxland, South Dakota - Cinnamon King, Manager
Augustana College, 2001 S. Summit Avenue
Room SS-44, Sioux Falls, ZIP: 57197
t: (605) 330-4264   *f:* (605) 330-4266

TENNESSEE
Memphis, Tennessee - Ree Russell, Manager
Buckman Hall, 650 East Parkway South, Suite 348
ZIP: 38104.
t: (901) 323-1543   *f:* (901) 320-9128

TEXAS - DALLAS
 LoRee Silloway, Director
P.O. Box 420069, ZIP: 75342-0069
2050 N. Stemmons Fwy., Suite 170, ZIP: 75207
t: (214) 767-0542   *f:* (214) 767-8240

UTAH
Salt Lake City, Utah - Stanley Rees, Director
324 S. State Street, Suite 221, ZIP: 84111
t: (801) 524-5116   *f:* (801) 524-5886

VERMONT
Montpelier, Vermont - Susan Murray, Manager
National Life Building, Drawer 20, ZIP: 05620-0501
t: (802) 828-4508   *f:* (802) 828-3258

VIRGINIA
Richmond, Virginia - Helen D. Lee Hwang, Manager
400 North 8th Street, Suite 540, ZIP: 23240-0026
P.O. Box 10026
t: (804) 771-2246   *f:* (804) 771-2390

WASHINGTON - SEATTLE
David Spann, Director
2001 6th Ave, Suite 650, ZIP: 98121
t: (206) 553-5615   *f:* (206) 553-7253

A3

WEST VIRGINIA

Charleston, West Virginia - Harvey Timberlake, Director
405 Capitol Street, Suite 807, ZIP: 25301
t: (304) 347-5123   *f:* (304) 347-5408

WISCONSIN

Milwaukee, Wisconsin - Paul D. Churchill, Director
517 E. Wisconsin Avenue, Room 596, ZIP: 53202
t: (414) 297-3473   *f:* (414) 297-3470

WYOMING

Served by the Denver, Colorado U.S. Export Assistance
Center

A3

Gorilla Guides

128 Kensington Church Street, London W8 4BH
Tel: (44) 207 221 7166; Fax: (44) 207 792 9288
E-mail: enquiries@stacey-international.co.uk

business travellers'
HANDBOOKS

The series that focuses on the needs of the business traveller

The Series

- **Unique:** Nothing like this currently available in the trade market
- **Recognised:** Already widely accepted as the reference by some chambers of commerce and export desks of The Department of Trade and Industry
- **Authoritative:** Highly experienced authors with extensive business experience in the target market

The Business Travellers' Guides to

- **Turkey**
- **Egypt**
- **Argentina**
- **The United Arab Emirates**
- **Saudi Arabia**

Content

- **Quality and Efficiency:** Essential tips on where to stay and how to get started
- **Etiquette:** The social morés of the local business culture
- **Creating an Impression:** Where to lunch and dine a local guest; basic vocabulary and phrases
- **The nitty-gritty:** Full details of organisations offering support and advice
- **Business Overviews:** Authoritative insights into the major economic and commercial sectors
- **Contacts:** Appendixes of useful contact details